The World's Best Hot Hatches Coloring Book

Pro Edition

Alexander Watts

Copyright 2020 - All Rights Reserved.

The content of this book may not be reproduced, duplicated, or transmitted without direct written permission from the author.

Under no circumstances will any legal responsibility or blame be held against the publisher for any reparation, damages, or monetary loss due to the information herein, either directly or indirectly.

Legal Notice:
You cannot amend, distribute, sell, use, quote or paraphrase any part of the content within this book without the consent of the author.

Disclaimer Notice:
Please note the information contained within this document is for educational and entertainment purpuses only. No warranties of any kind are expressed or implied. Readers acknowledge that the author is not engaging in the rendering of legal, financial, medical or professional advice.

Contents

- Simca 1100Ti (1974)
- Volkswagen Golf GTI Mk1 (1976)
- Talbot Sunbeam Lotus (1979)
- Renault 5 Turbo 2 (1983)
- Peugeot 205 1.9 GTI (1986)
- Lancia Delta Integrale Evolution II (1993)
- Renault Clio Williams (1993)
- Renault Clio V6 Phase 2 (2003)
- MINI JCW GP (2006)
- Renault Mégane R26.R (2009)
- Ford Focus RS500 (2010)
- Honda Civic Type-R (FK8 model from 2017)

With each of the cars, you'll learn a bit about what makes them so special and why they have made the final cut for the 'The World's Best Hot Hatches Coloring Book'.

There's also some of the very important stats that are essential in benchmarking each car against its competitors in the hot hatch segment.

With each car there is also a small test picture so you can check your color choice before you get stuck into the main drawings. Once you have completed your masterpiece, why don't you carefully cut out your picture and frame it and put it on your wall? Or maybe send to a close relative? Whatever you decide, I hope you get hours of coloring pleasure and that you can learn about these wonderful cars to appreciate them, just as I do!

Foreword

Hello, and a very warm welcome to you and thanks for purchasing this coloring book!

Cars have long been a passion of mine ever since I was a kid. When I was younger, I used to have pictures of the quintessential supercars of the era - Lamborghini Countaches and Porsche 911s both adorned the limited space I had available on my wall.

One of the more 'real world' categories of car that, perhaps, many more of the demographic might actually be able to own, are 'Hot Hatches'. A hot hatch (short for hot hatchback) is a high-performance version of an otherwise 'normal' mass produced hatchback vehicle.

So, who made the first hot hatch? Many people believe this to be the Volkswagen Golf GTI which was first launched in 1976 in Europe. The VW Golf (called Rabbit GTI in the U.S. & Canada and VW Caribe GT in Mexico) was possibly the first widely recognised hot hatch, however, there were a few other models of the early '70s that could possibly have started the whole hot hatch era.

The BMW 2000 tii Touring was possibly a good early contender for the title as it offered the right ingredients of a more powerful engine with a lifting hatchback! There was also the 1971 Autobianchi A112 Abarth which offered most of the elements of what a hot hatch was all about. The A112, however, only managed to squeeze out a fairly puny 58hp from its 982cc engine so it might be considered more of a 'lukewarm' hatch as opposed to something approaching 'hot'. So, many view the Simca 1100TI to be the first of its breed. It was a traditional functional hatchback that received a twin-carb engine, bigger brakes and stiffer shocks - the essential ingredients for a car with a greater focus on speed. The Simca 1100TI was good for a 0-60 time of just under 12 seconds and a max speed of 105mph. This may not seem like a great deal of performance by today's standards, but back in 1973 this would have left many cars eating its dust.

So, with the market starting to realize that there was a big demand for these 'regular' hatchbacks that went a lot faster than their cooler (less fast!) counterparts the 'Hot Hatch' era was born!

I hope you enjoy the selection of cars that I have included in this coloring book and that you can learn a bit about their origins with the accompanying detail that supports each car.

Happy coloring,

Alex W

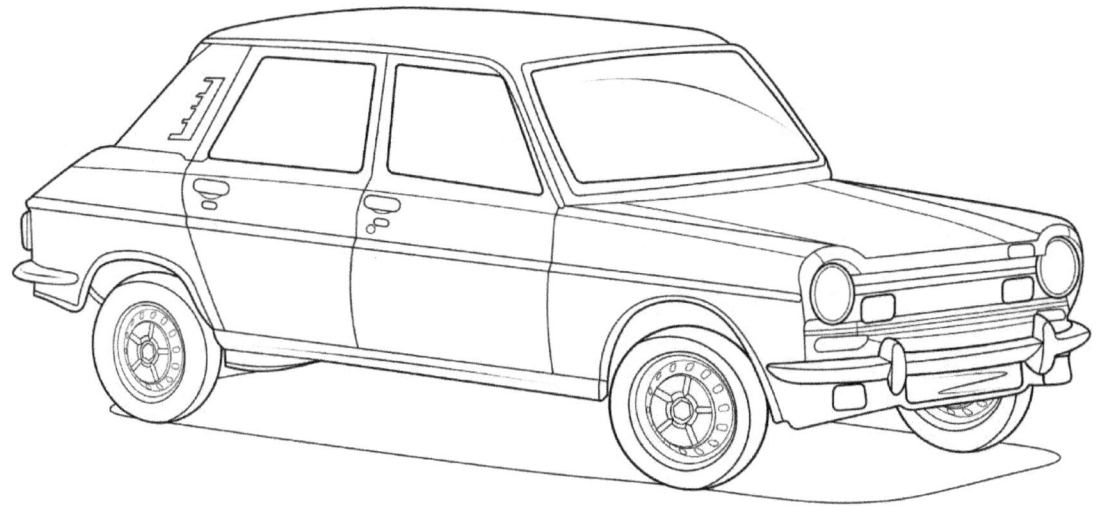

Simca 1100Ti (1974)

So, let's kick things off with a hot hatch that many consider to be car that started the whole hot hatch segment – the Simca 1100Ti from 1974.

Simca (Société Industrielle de Mécanique et Carrosserie Automobile) were a French car maker whose origins date back to 1934. In 1970 they became a subsidiary of Chrysler Group and remained as a recognised manufacturer until 1978 until Chrysler divested their European operations to PSA Peugeot Citroen. At this point PSA replaced any Simca badged models with Simca-Talbot badging.

The Simca 1100 Ti was based on the regular 1100 'Special' which was first introduced in 1970. The Ti got a 6 headlight and foglight arrangement, front and rear spoilers, front disc brakes, matte black grille, alloy wheels and a single color paint scheme. This was then to become the hot hatch recipe for many other manufacturers to follow. A front engine layout with front wheel drive was the preferred power delivery option as this was a more economical way of car production whilst simultaneously optimising efficiency and passenger space for its passengers, however, there are many other formats to engine and power delivery options as we will find out later in this book!

Engine Size:	1,294 cc / 79.0 cu in
Power:	81 bhp
0-60:	11.9 seconds
Max Speed:	105 mph
Weight:	918 kg / 2,024 lbs

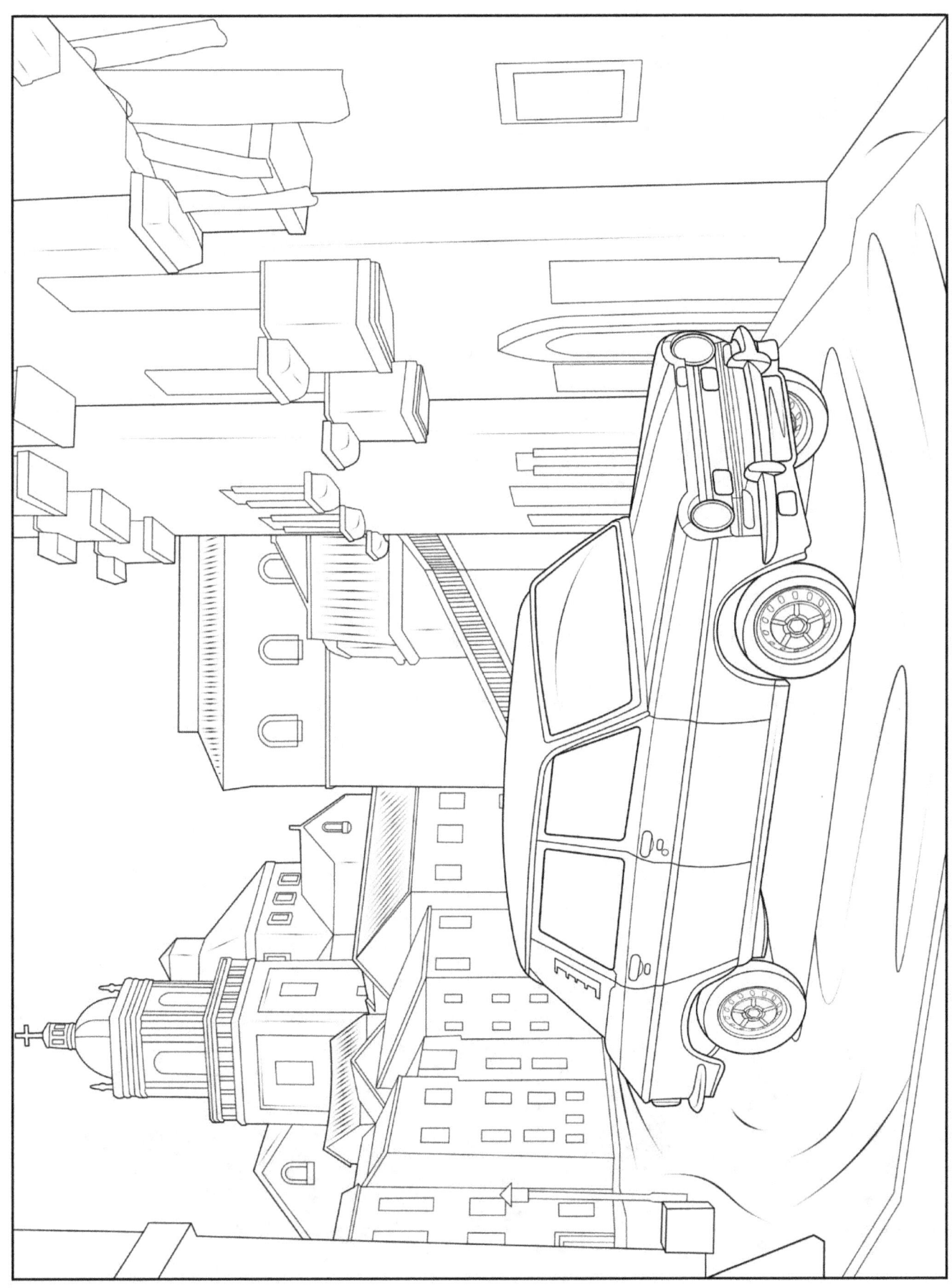

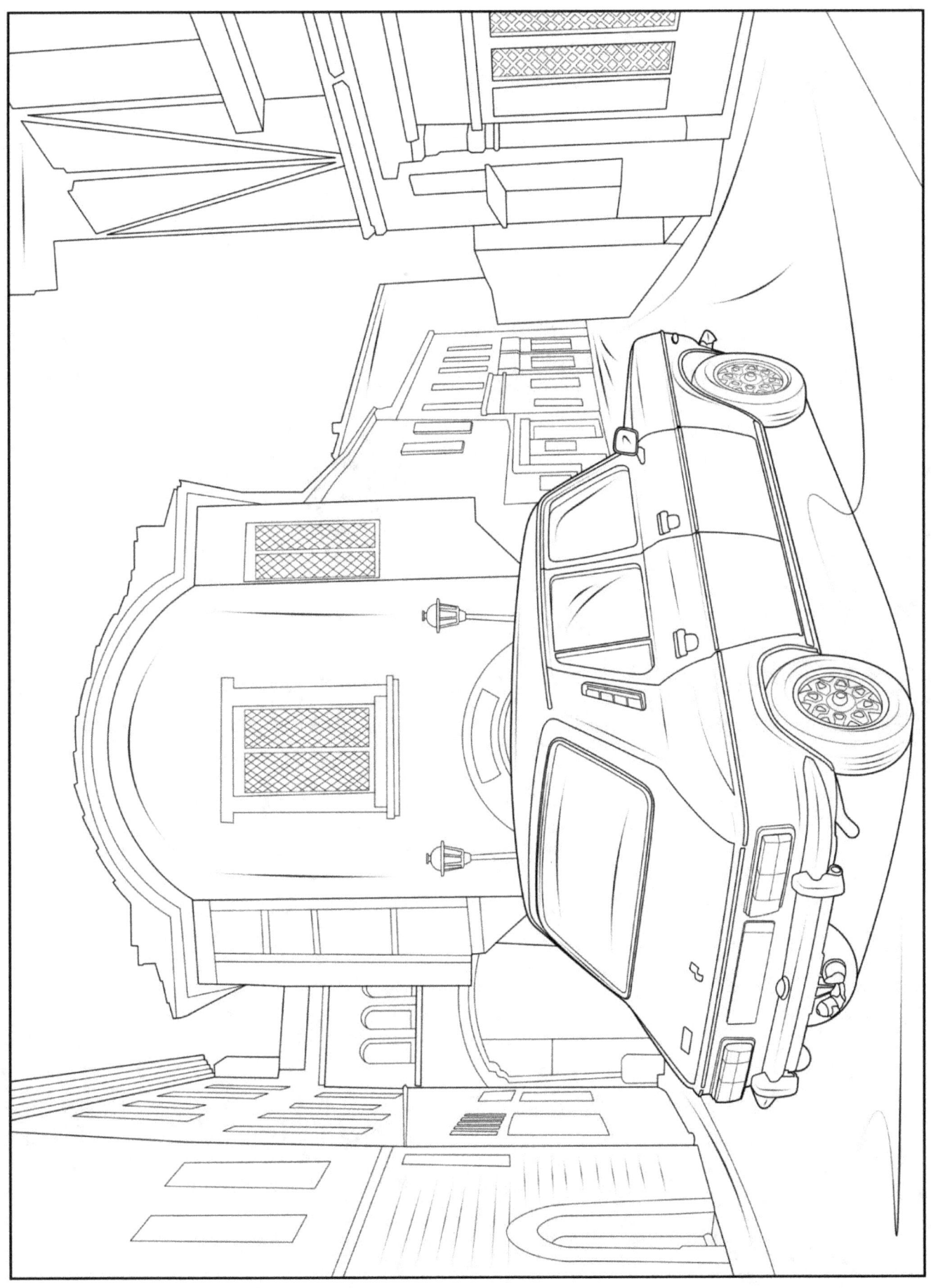

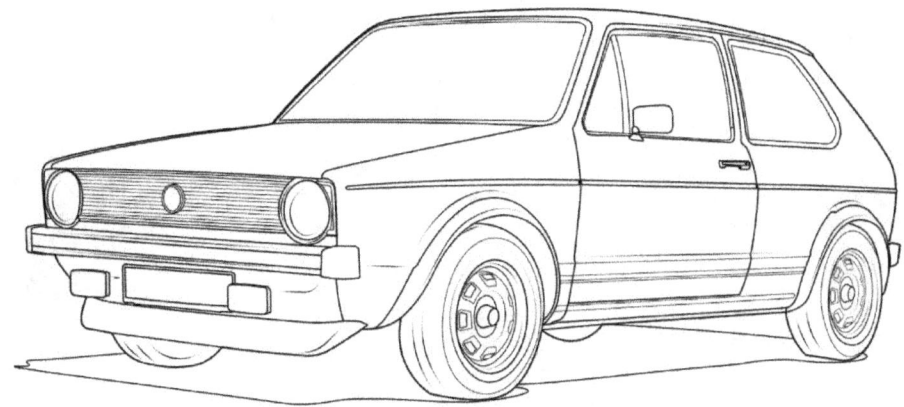

Volkswagen Golf GTI MK1 (1976)

The next hot hatch in our line-up is, perhaps, the most well-known and well received hot hatch of all time - the original VW Golf GTI Mk1 (Grand Tourer Injection).

Having received somewhat negative reactions towards the Beetle GSR (Gelb-Schwarzer Renner or 'Yellow-Black Racer') VW initially had little inclination to develop a fast version of the Golf. The original prototype Golf GTI was described by VW's chief of research as 'undriveable' due to its twin carburettors and lowered and stiffened suspension. A decision was then taken to use a Bosch fuel injected system to reduce the noise and increase the power – it was at this point that the phrase 'GTI' was born.

The Golf is known as a 'Rabbit' in the U.S. and Canada, a Citi Golf in South Africa and as the VW Caribe (meaning Caribbean) in Mexico. There have been several different body styles throughout the lifespan of the Golf too which include a pickup (also known as a "Caddy"), a Cabriolet, an Estate/Wagon and as a saloon/sedan (badged as a VW Jetta). There have also been several limited-edition models along the way too.

The Golf GTI is now entering into its eight generation and remains as one of the most popular hot hatches in the world.

Engine Size: 1,588 cc / 96.9 cu in
Power: 108 bhp
0-60:   8.9 seconds
Max Speed: 113 mph
Weight: 810 kg / 1,786 lbs

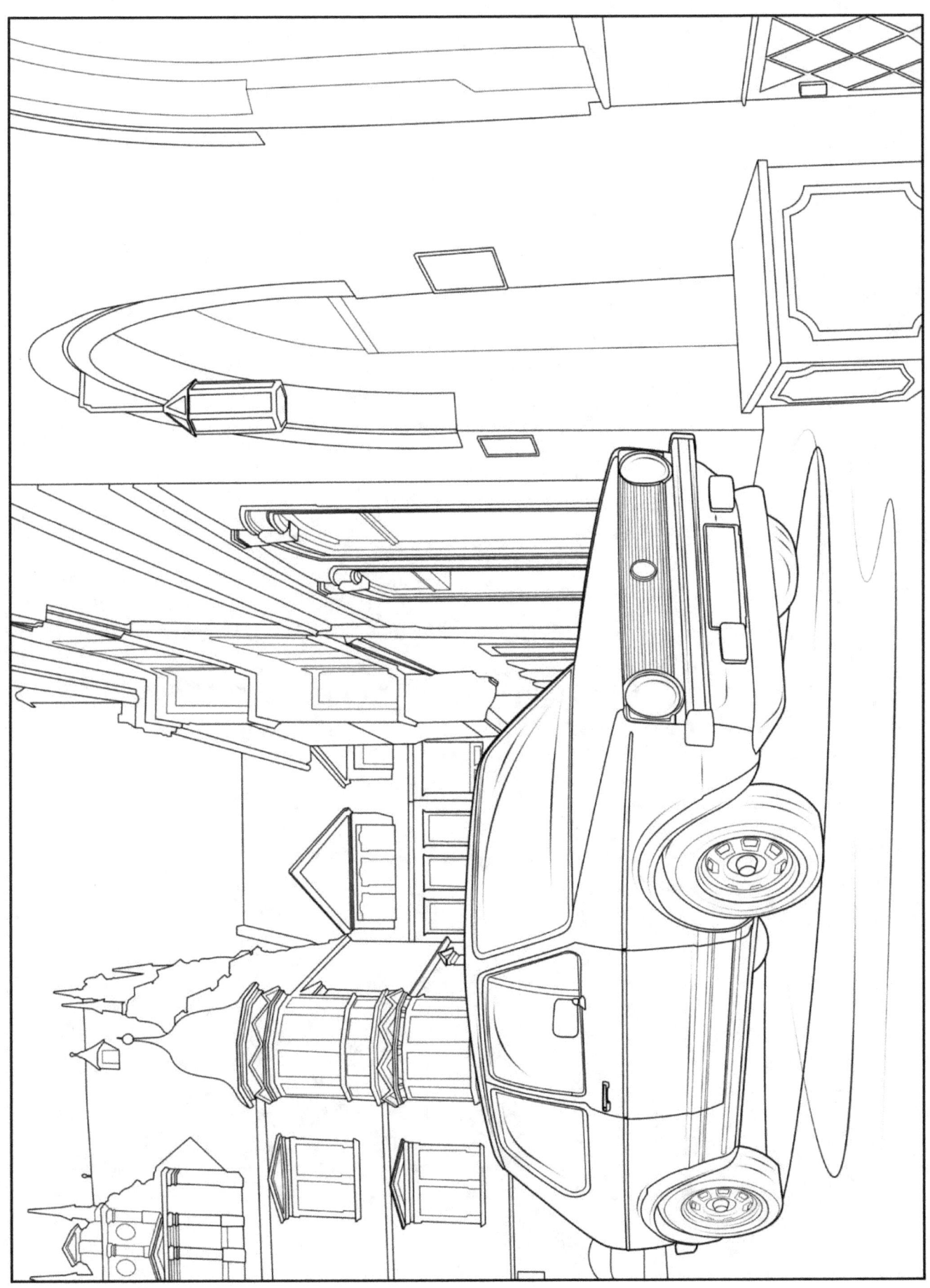

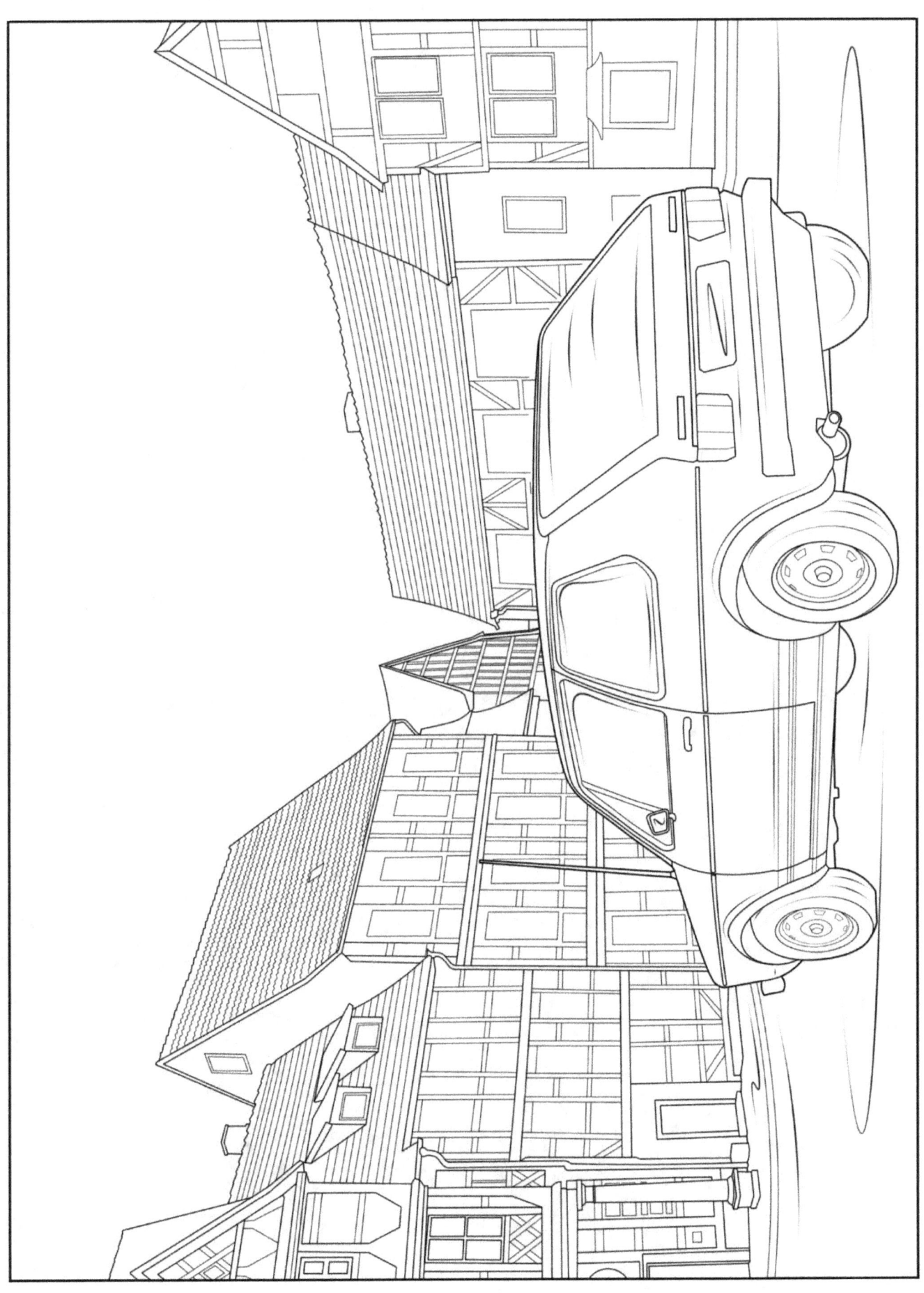

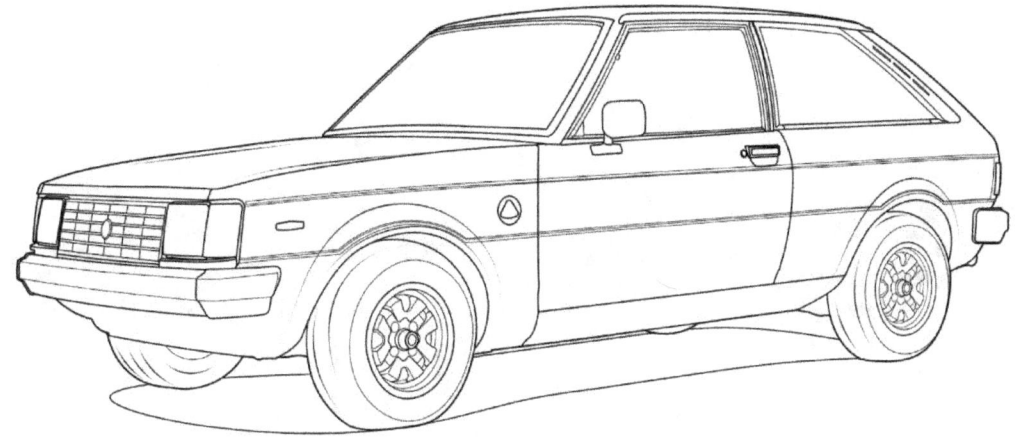

Talbot Sunbeam Lotus (1979)

In the mid '70s the British automotive industry was going through troubled times. Chrysler's main competitor, British Leyland were nationalised, and the Chrysler management team thought that they too would try and benefit from state assistance. The UK government agreed, and this afforded Chrysler with a grant reported to be £55 million to help fund the development of a small hatchback model to fill a gap in the market. A tight schedule, a somewhat limited budget and the requirement to mainly use UK sourced parts meant that the Sunbeam was developed using the platform of a rear wheel drive Hillman Avenger rather than a more en vogue front wheel drive set up.

The Sunbeam was only ever available as a three-door variant and one of its main design features was a rear hatch formed from a single piece of glass.

The hot version came later in 1979 in the form of a Sunbeam Ti and, in its ultimate guise, as the Talbot Lotus Sunbeam. The Lotus Sunbeam models were engineered with a 2,172 cc Lotus engine which was specially developed for this car. The Talbot Lotus Sunbeam proved to be a rally success in '80 and '81 bringing the manufacturer's championship to Talbot.

Engine Size: 2,172 cc / 132.5 cu in
Power: 150 bhp
0-60: 7.4 seconds
Max Speed: 121 mph
Weight: 960 kg / 2,116 lbs

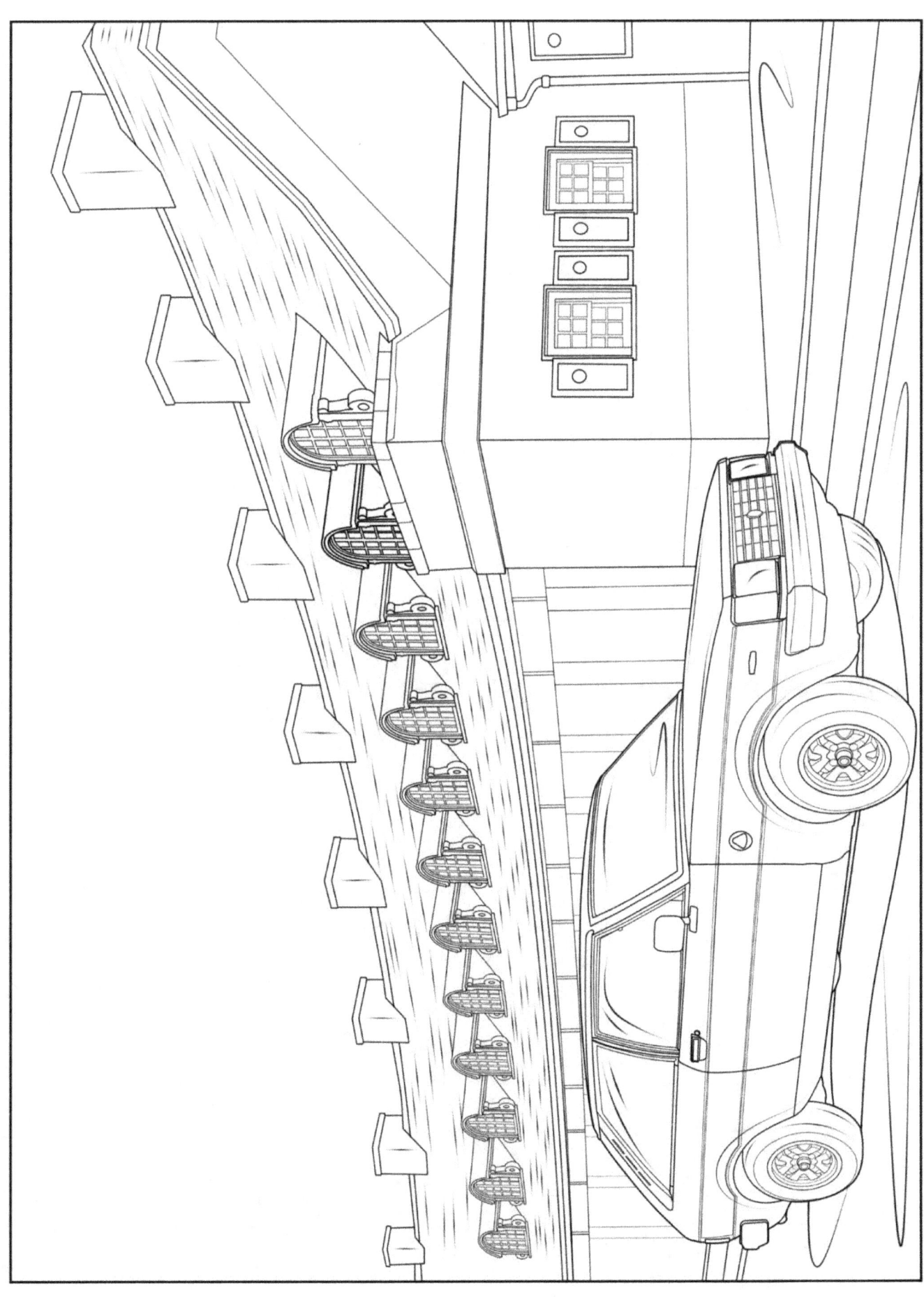

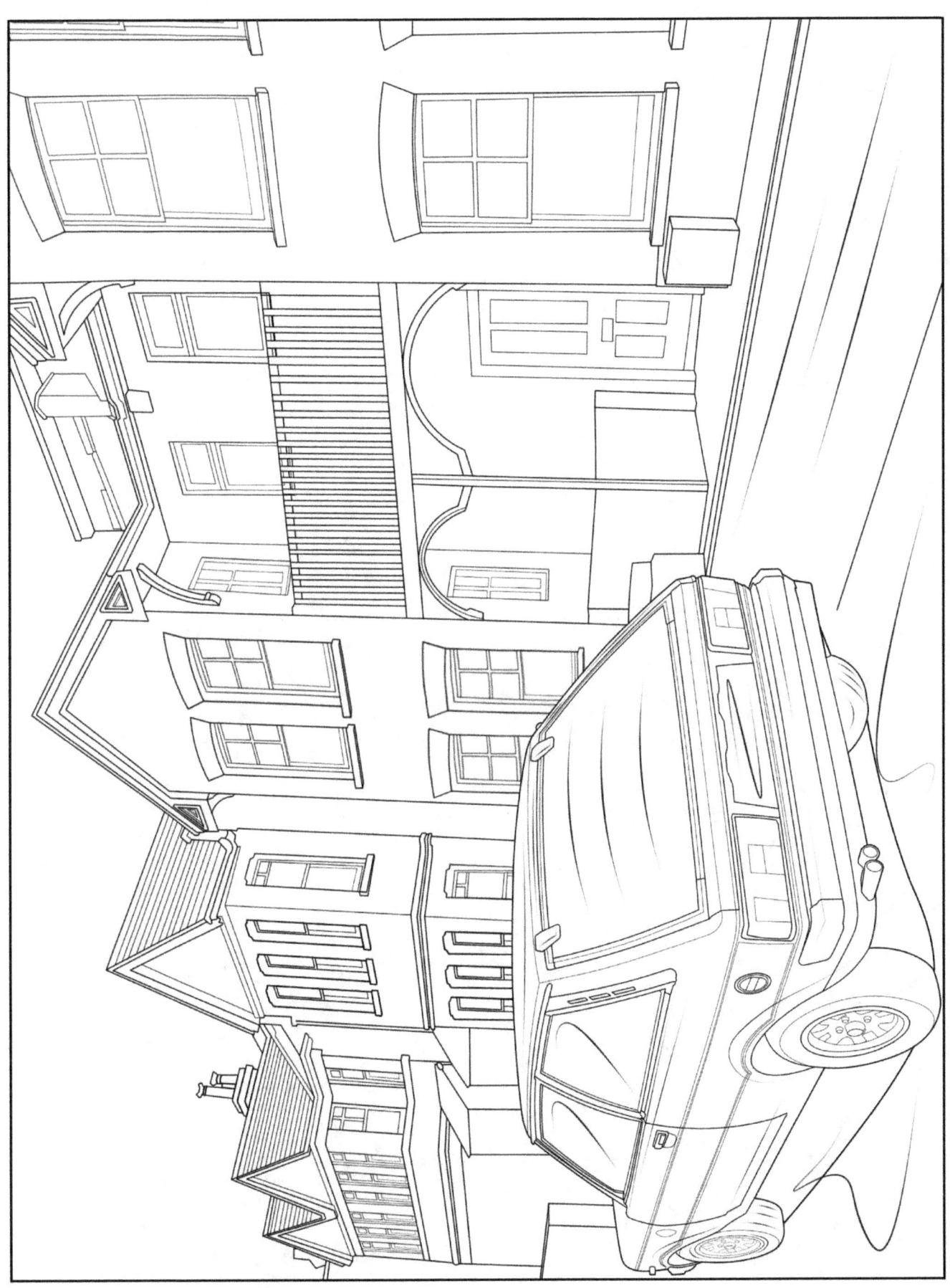

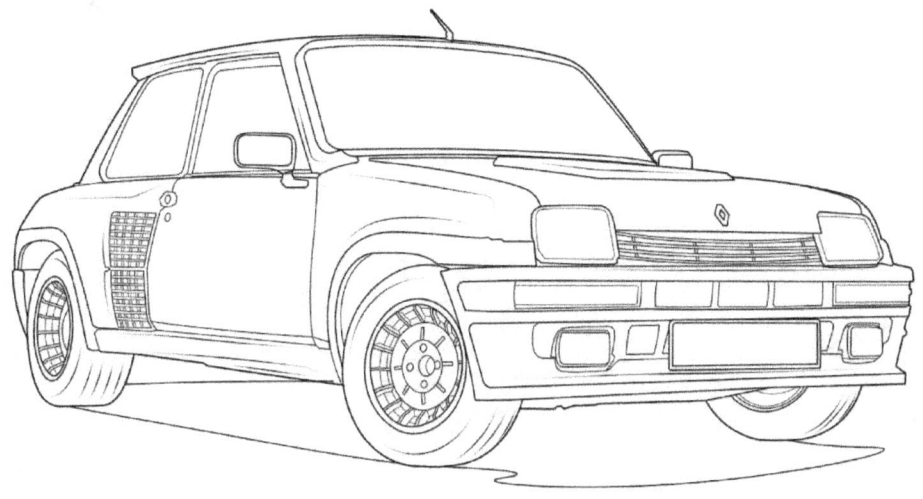

Renault 5 Turbo 2 (1983)

In 1983 Renault took things up several notches when they released the Renault 5 Turbo 2. The standard R5 (known in the US as an AMC 'Le Car') was a front engine front wheel drive model. The Renault 5 Turbo and Turbo 2 models took their inspiration from Group B rally cars of the era and used a mid-engine with rear wheel drive set up. The engine was a Bosch fuel injected 1,397 cc 4-cylinder unit coupled with a Garrett T3 turbocharger in place or where the rear seats would normally have been located.

The Turbo 2 model was the second generation of the R5 Turbo and was launched in 1983. It used more of the regular stock parts from the Renault 5 Alpine. The Turbo 2 offered similar levels of performance compared to its predecessor but was about 25% less expensive.

The Renault 5 Turbo experienced great success in its rallying career including a win at the Monte Carlo Rally in 1981 which was also its first outing in the World Rally Championship.

R5 Turbos are hugely desirable and command very high prices by collectors.

Engine Size: 1,397 cc turbo / 85.3 cu in
Power: 158 bhp
0-60:   6.7 seconds
Max Speed: 126 mph
Weight: 970 kg / 2,138 lbs

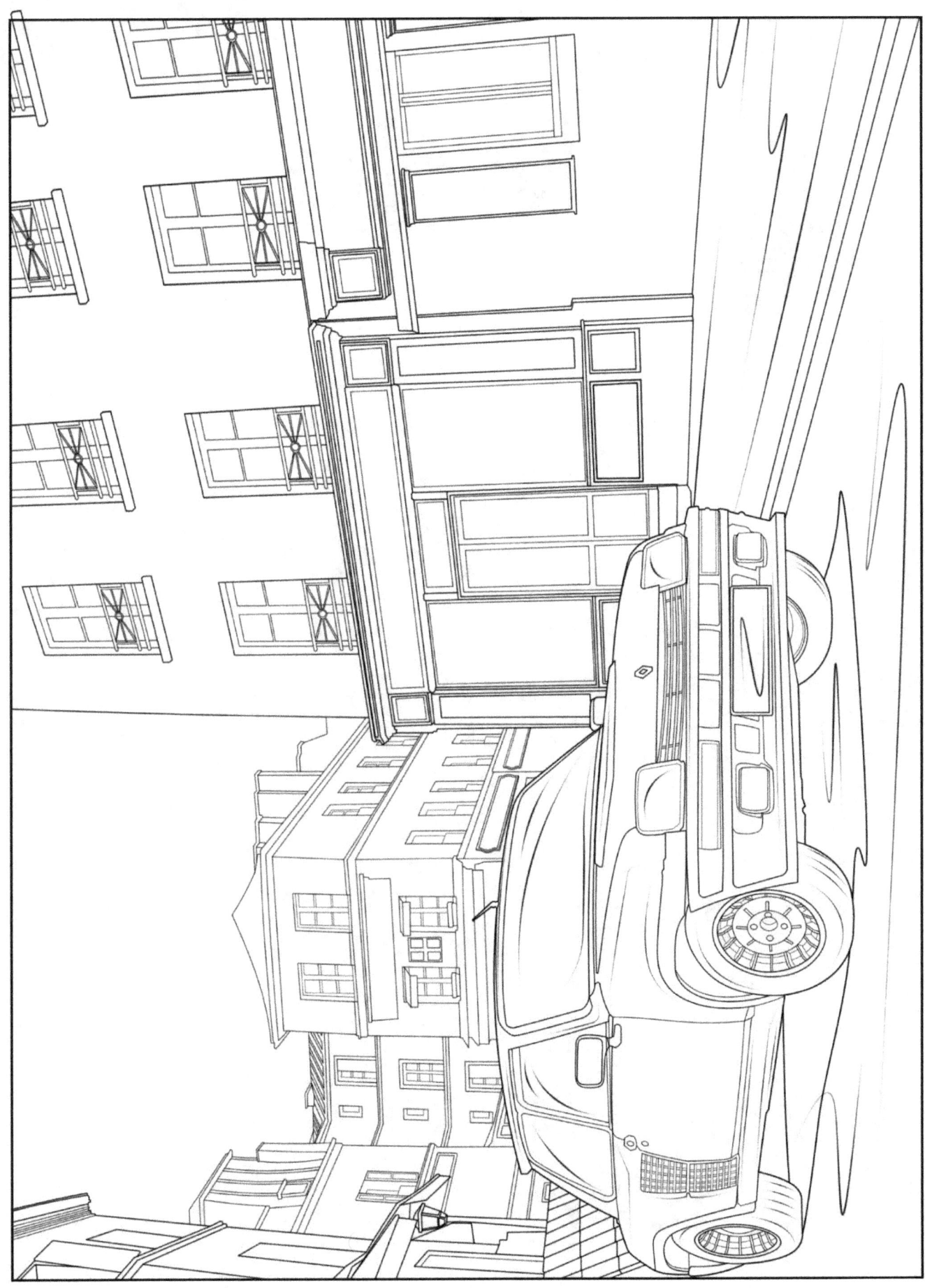

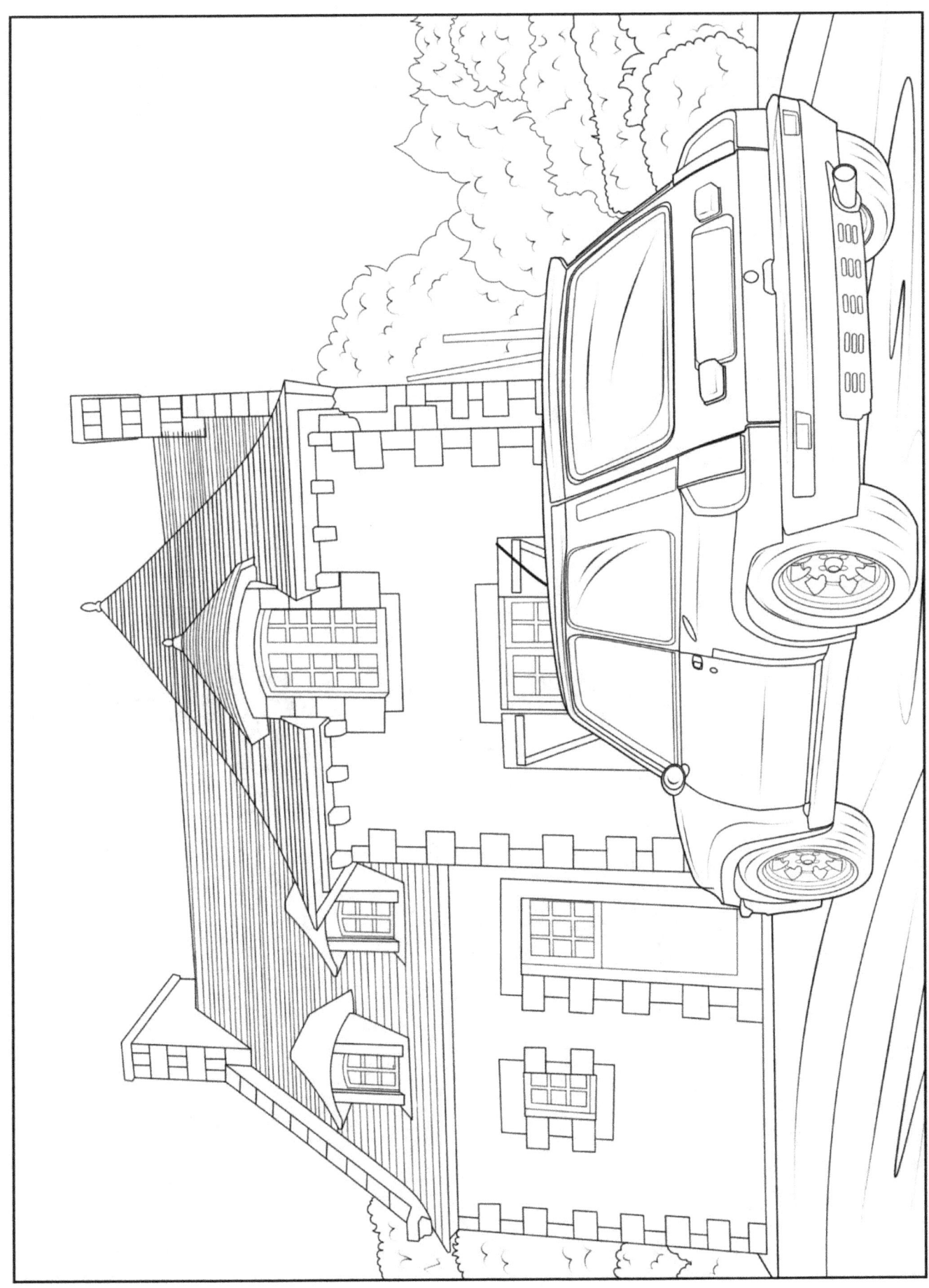

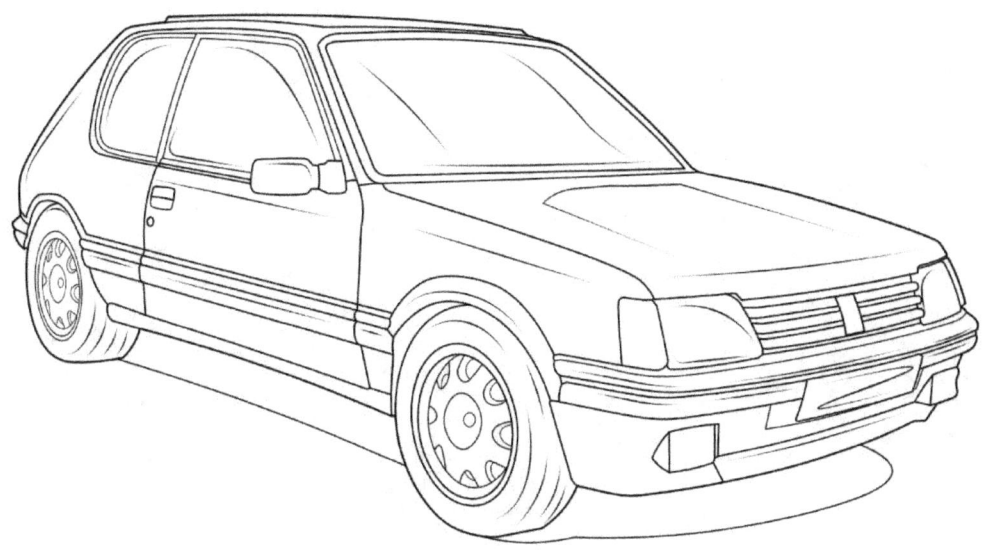

Peugeot 205 1.9 GTI (1986)

The Peugeot 205 was built as the successor to the Peugeot 104 which originally entered the market in 1973. Peugeot traditionally were considered to be a conservative manufacturer of larger sedan (saloon) vehicles, namely the 504 and the 505 station wagon models, however they really hit the mark with the 205 when it was launched in 1983. The foundations of the 205 originated with Peugeot's takeover of Chrysler's European division and Simca who had significant expertise in the manufacturing capabilities of small cars such as the Simca 1100 and the Hillman Imp (made in the U.K). It was this time that they started working on the 205.

In 1984 the Peugeot 205 1.6 GTI came along and it was powered by a 1,580 cc (96.4 cu in) four cylinder engine which generated a fairly modest 104 hp. Apart from a more powerful engine the 205 also received larger plastic wheel arches, bigger front and rear bumper valances, lowered stiffer suspension, drop-linked anti-roll bars and disc brakes at the front. In 1986 Peugeot introduced the 1.9 litre model into the market. The 1.9 litre model received a bigger engine which increased the power to 130 hp (later 1.9 models had their power reduced to 120 hp due to a catalytic convertor for emissions requirements), it also received half-leather seats, disc brakes all round and bigger 15" alloy wheels.

Opinion is still divided, to this day, between the 1.6 and 1.9 models. Many prefer the peaky power delivery of the 1.6, whilst many others prefer the more favourable torque delivery of the 1.9. Either way, the 205 remains as one of the best ever hot hatches of all time.

Engine Size:	1,905 cc / 116.3 cu in
Power:	128 bhp
0-60:	7.6 seconds
Max Speed:	128 mph
Weight:	875 kg / 1,929 lbs

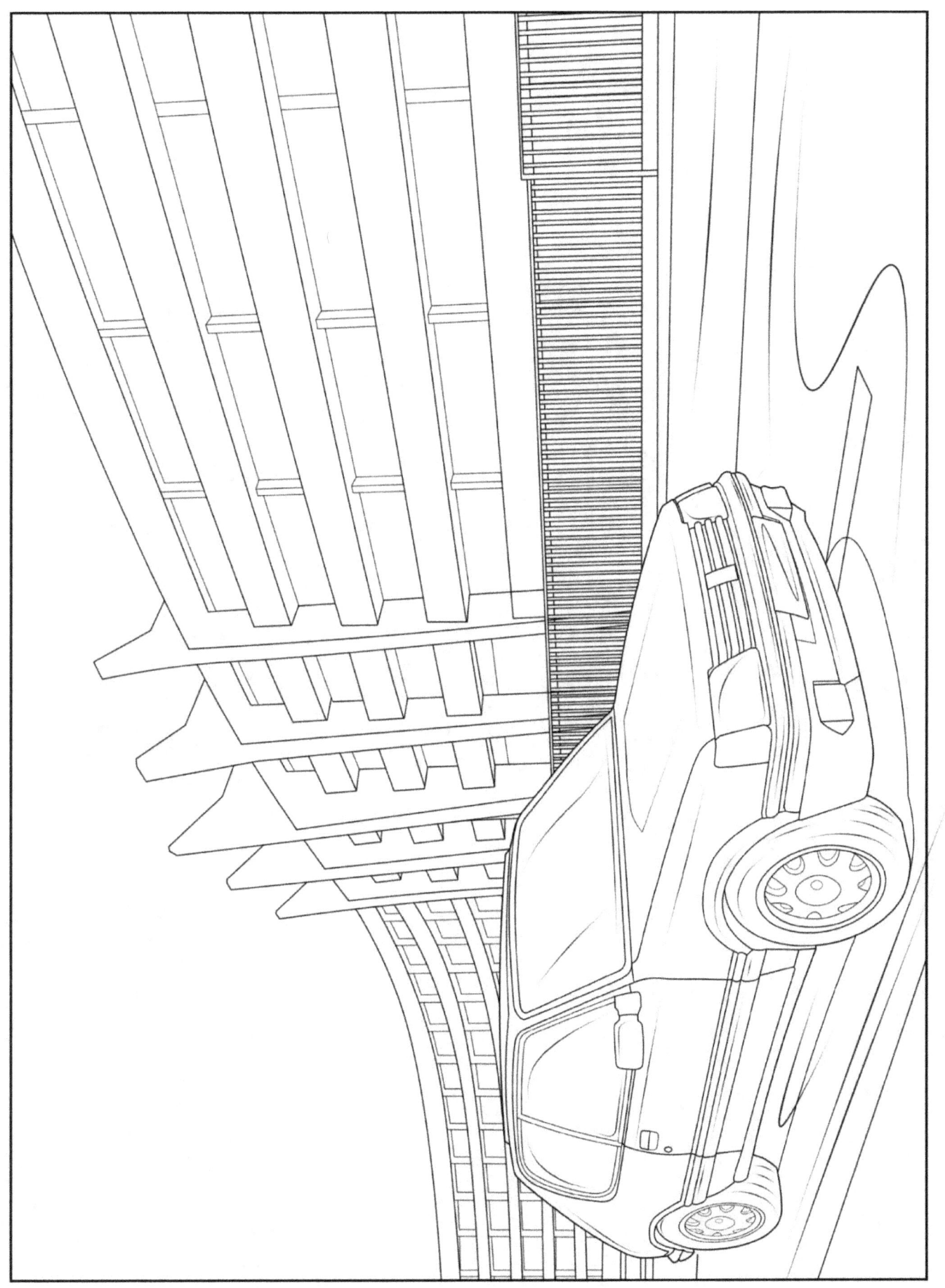

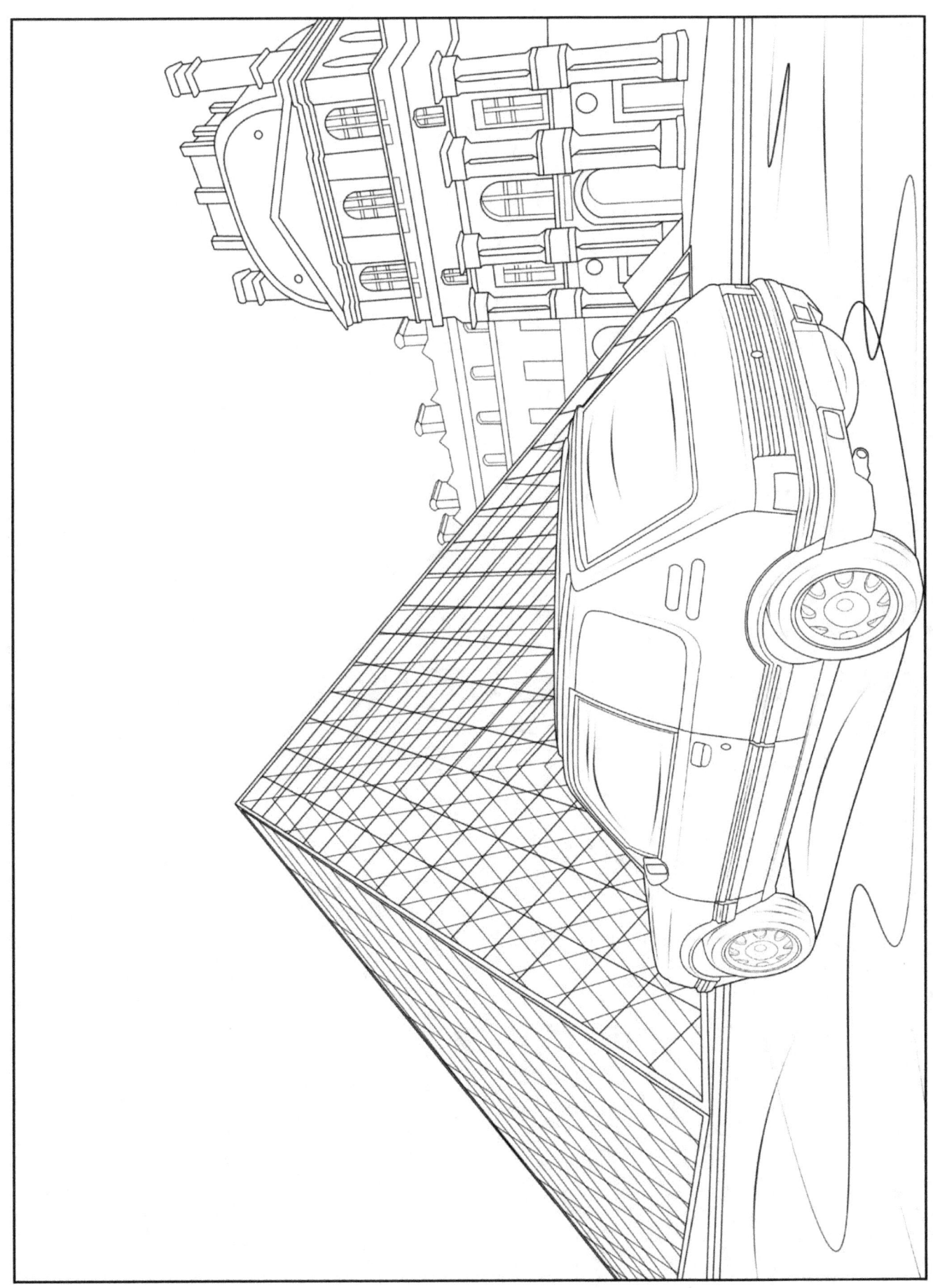

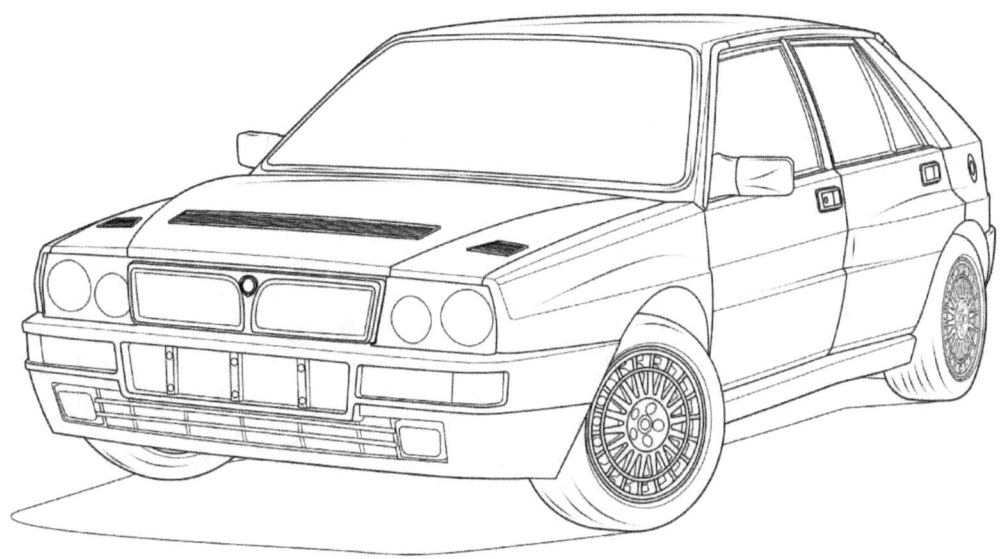

Lancia Delta Integrale Evolution II (1993)

The Lancia Delta was first released in 1979 and it was Lancia's first front wheel drive small car offering since the demise of its predecessor in 1973 – the Lancia Fulvia.

The first high performance models came in 1983 and were badged as 'HF' which stood for 'High Fidelity'. The HF moniker had been used previously for Lancia's racing variants from the mid '60s. In 1985 an HF Turbo model was added to the Delta model line-up. Many models were front wheel drive, but Lancia also offered their four-wheel drive option across several models in the Delta range.

It wasn't until 1991 that the first of the 'Evoluzione' (or simply 'Evo') models was first launched. This was also the same year that Lancia officially retired from rallying. Evo models received the full treatment of a power increase to the 2.0 litre turbocharged engine (with 207 hp), a wider front and rear track, Evo bodywork styling, larger alloy wheels, a manually adjustable roof spoiler, strengthened steering rack and re-worked suspension. It was basically a rally car, but for the road!

The Evo II arrived in 1993 and had yet more power which was up to 212 hp. It was the only Integrale model which wasn't raced. It was built in honor of the achievements of the rally version of the Delta. It came with some body modifications to distinguish it from the original Evo. It was limited to just three colors – Bianco (white), Rosso Monza (red) and Blu Lancia (dark blue). The Lancia Delta Integrale Evoluzione II's rallying heritage proved to be hugely popular then and they remain highly desirable today. A true hot hatchback rally legend!

Engine Size: 1,995 cc / 121.7 cu in
Power: 212 bhp
0-60:   5.7 seconds
Max Speed: 137 mph
Weight: 1,340 kg / 2,954 lbs

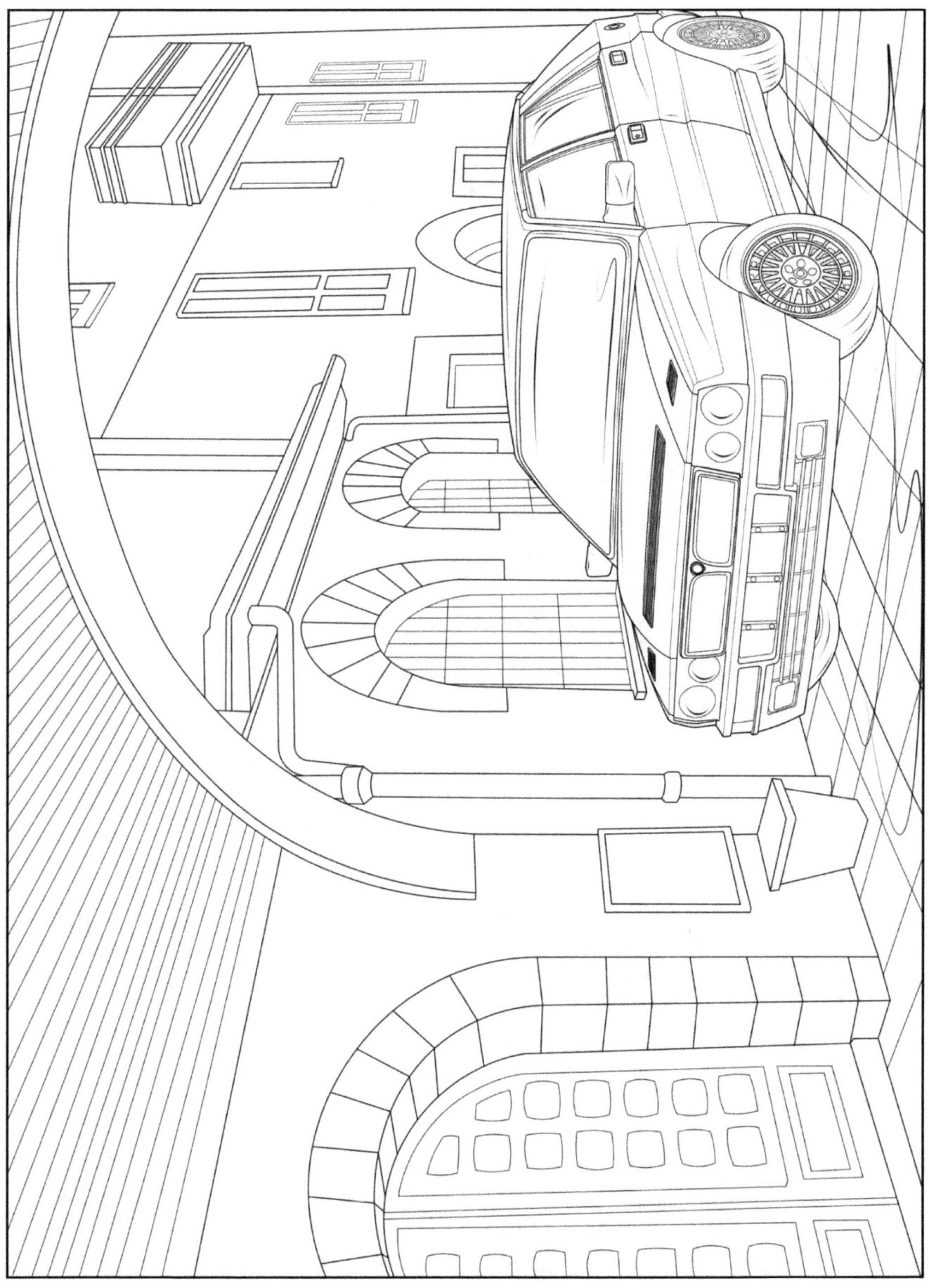

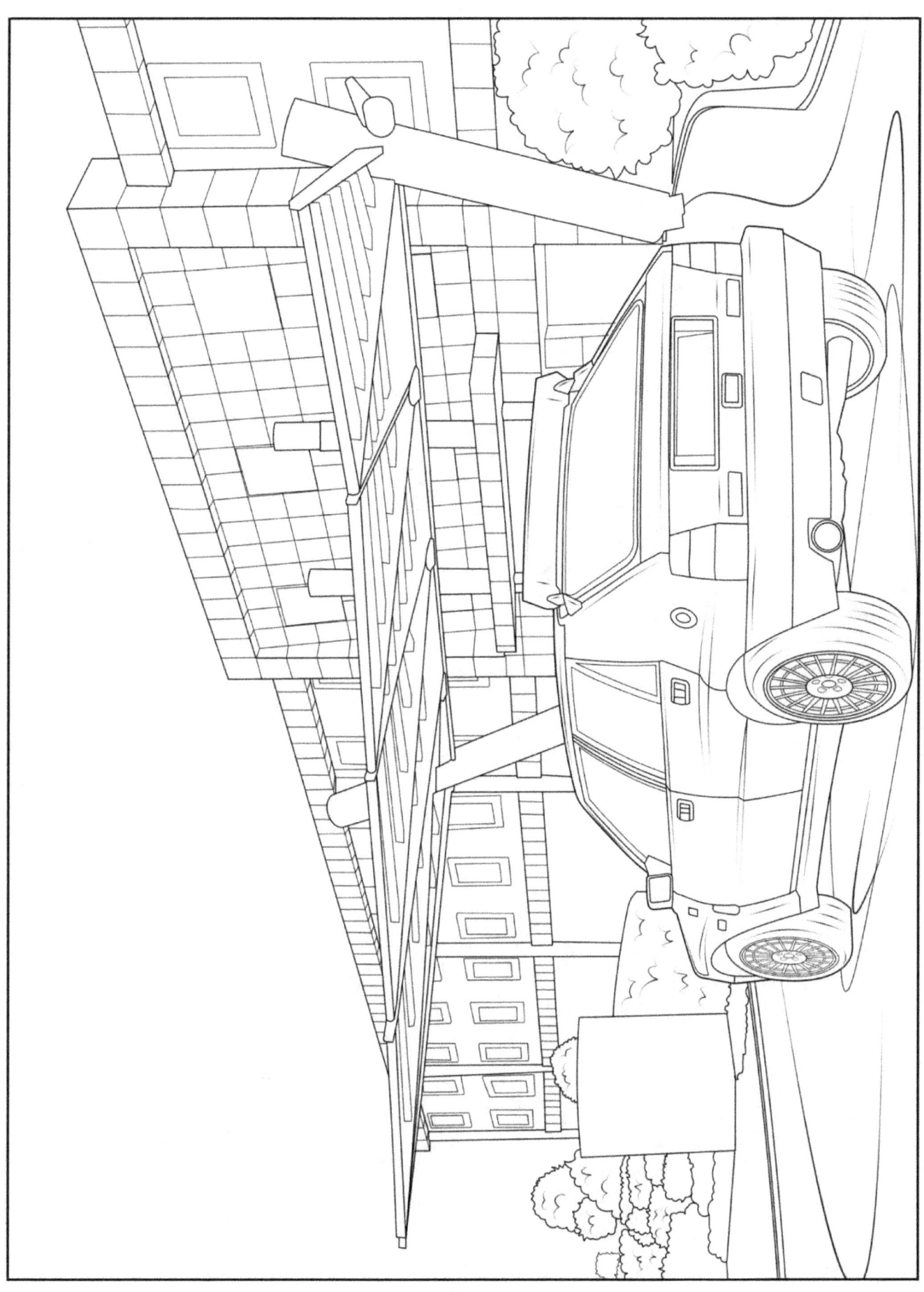

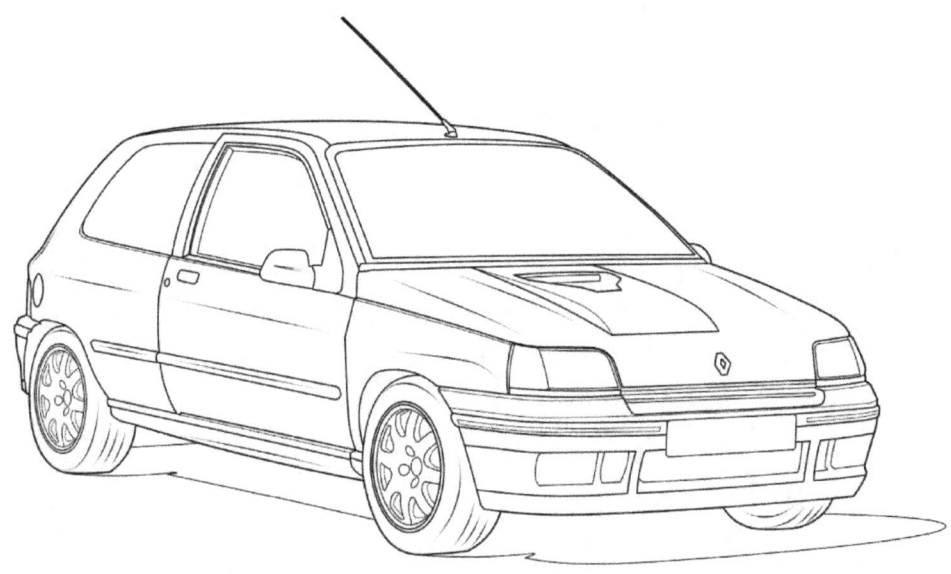

Renault Clio Williams (1993)

In the early '90s the title for the hot hatch crown was wrestled mainly between the 1.8 litre Clio 16v and the aforementioned Peugeot 205 1.9 GTI. Both set the standard for looks, handling and performance in this sector. With the addition of the Clio Williams in 1993 (the name derived from its association with the F1 team), the bar got raised again and the Williams stole the crown. The Clio Williams was a homologation model with 3,800 models initially (1,300 more than the minimum requirement). These all sold out, so Renault made another 1,600 more.

The Clio Williams received a normally aspirated 2.0 litre engine with uprated springs, dampers and rear torsion arms and thicker anti-roll bars. The external upgrades were wider arches and a power bulge on the hood (bonnet). The most notable feature on the Williams model were the stunningly beautiful 15" gold alloy wheels!

The Clio Williams models were so popular that Renault decided to make a Williams 2 and eventually a Williams 3 much to the annoyance of the original Williams customers who were told that the car would only be built in limited numbers to protect resale values. The original Williams models had individually numbered plaques, but the Williams 2 & 3 did not.

The Clio Williams remains as one of the most easily distinguishable hot hatches from the '90s and are one of the most rewarding hot hatches to drive. The performance figures when the car was originally launched are impressive by today's standards – these must have been an absolute thing of wonder back in 1993.

Engine Size:	1,998 cc / 121.9 cu in
Power:	145 bhp
0-60:	7.6 seconds
Max Speed:	134 mph
Weight:	981 kg / 2,163 lbs

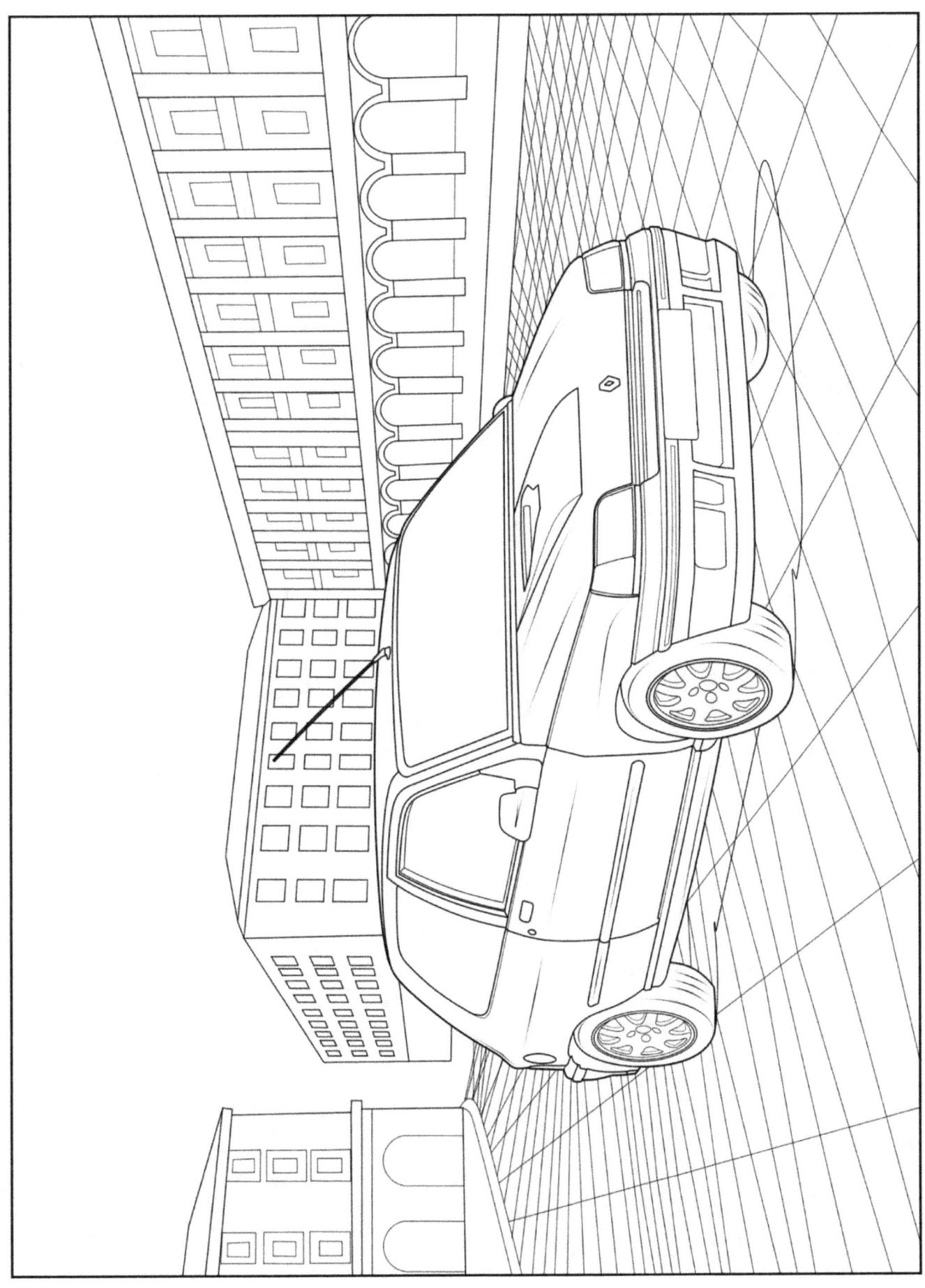

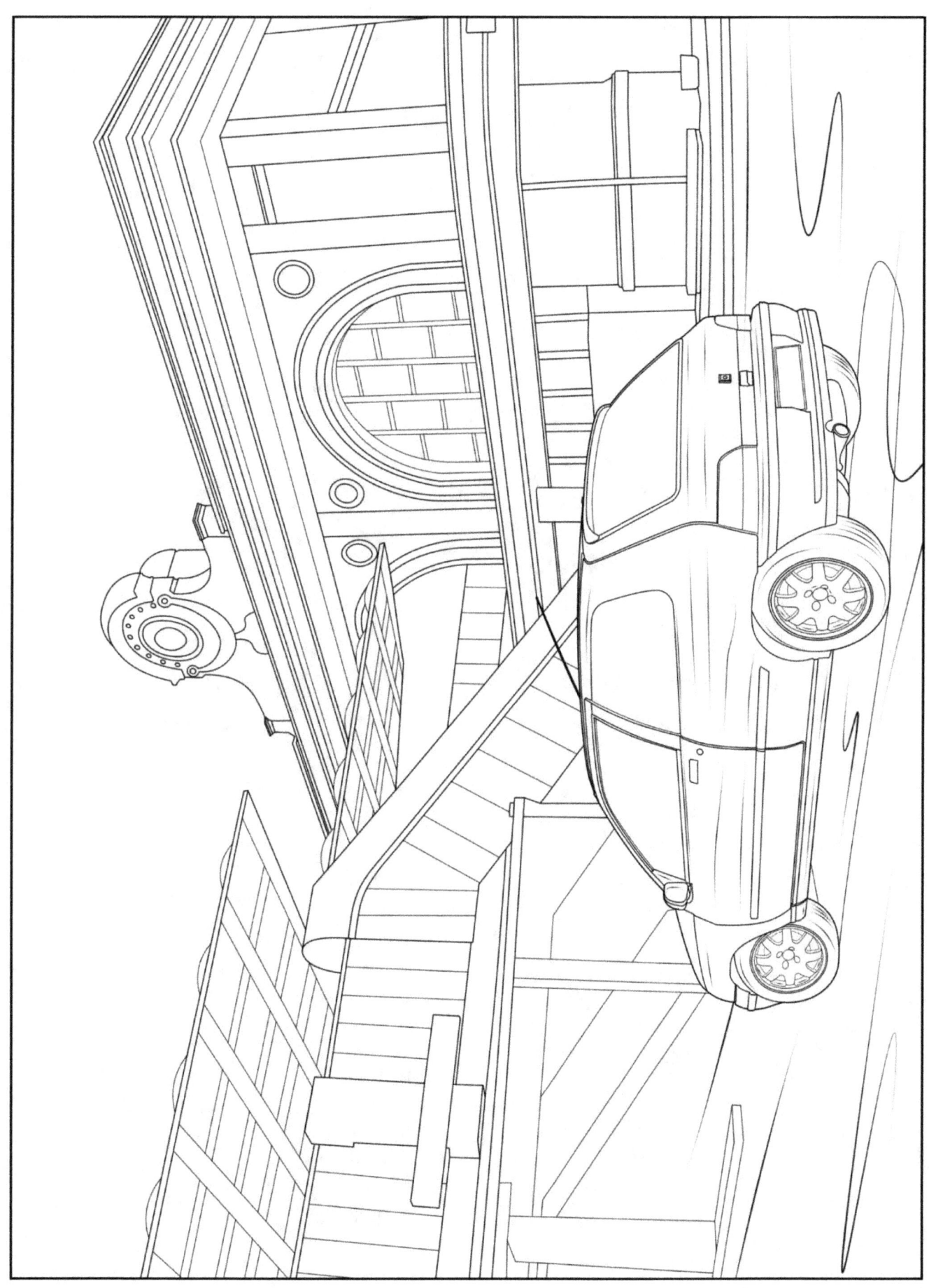

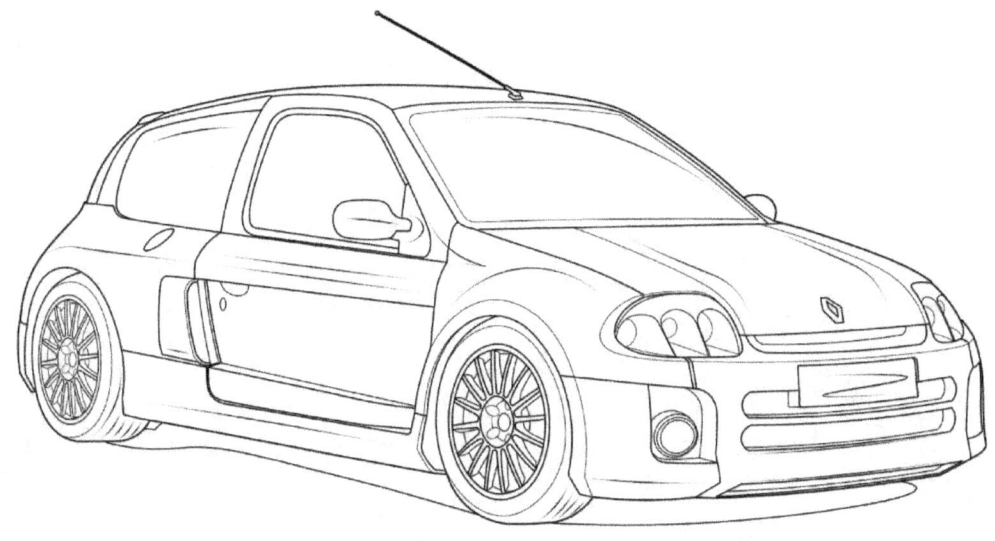

Renault Sport Clio V6 Phase 2 (2003)

The Renault Clio V6 was a rear engine hot hatch with a rear wheel drive layout that somehow managed to get sign off by Renault's bean counters.

The first Clio V6 was launched in 2001 and was co-developed between Renault Sport and Tom Walkinshaw Racing (TWR). Inspiration came from the Renault 5 Turbo as the V6 was fully re-worked and the Renault Laguna sourced engine (with power increased with the help of Porsche engineers) was placed in the centre of the car behind the front seats. Despite having been significantly re-engineered the Clio V6 was 300kg heavier than the next sportiest Clio in the range – the Clio 172.

With the extra weight of the six-cylinder engine there was only a marginal improvement in acceleration compared to the Clio 172 model, however, the Clio V6 did manage a significantly higher top speed.

The Clio V6, when driven in the wet, would have to be driven with the utmost of respect or it would punish the unskilled heavily. That aside, as an exercise of desirability, it remains hugely desirable and one of the best cars that Renault has ever produced.

There were 2,822 Clio V6's produced.

Engine Size:	2,946 cc / 179.8 cu in
Power:	252 bhp
0-60:	5.9 seconds
Max Speed:	153 mph
Weight:	1,400 kg / 3,086 lbs

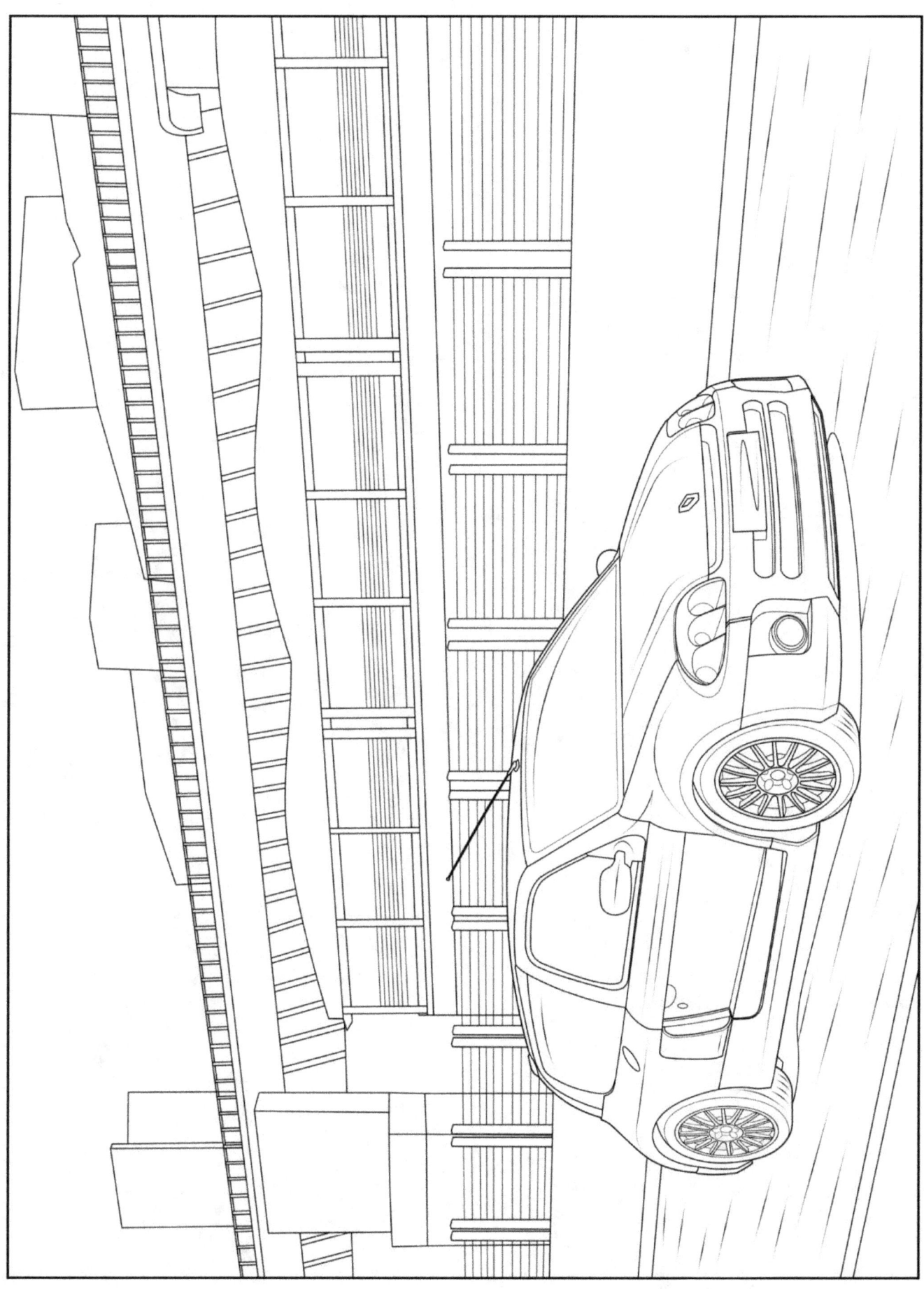

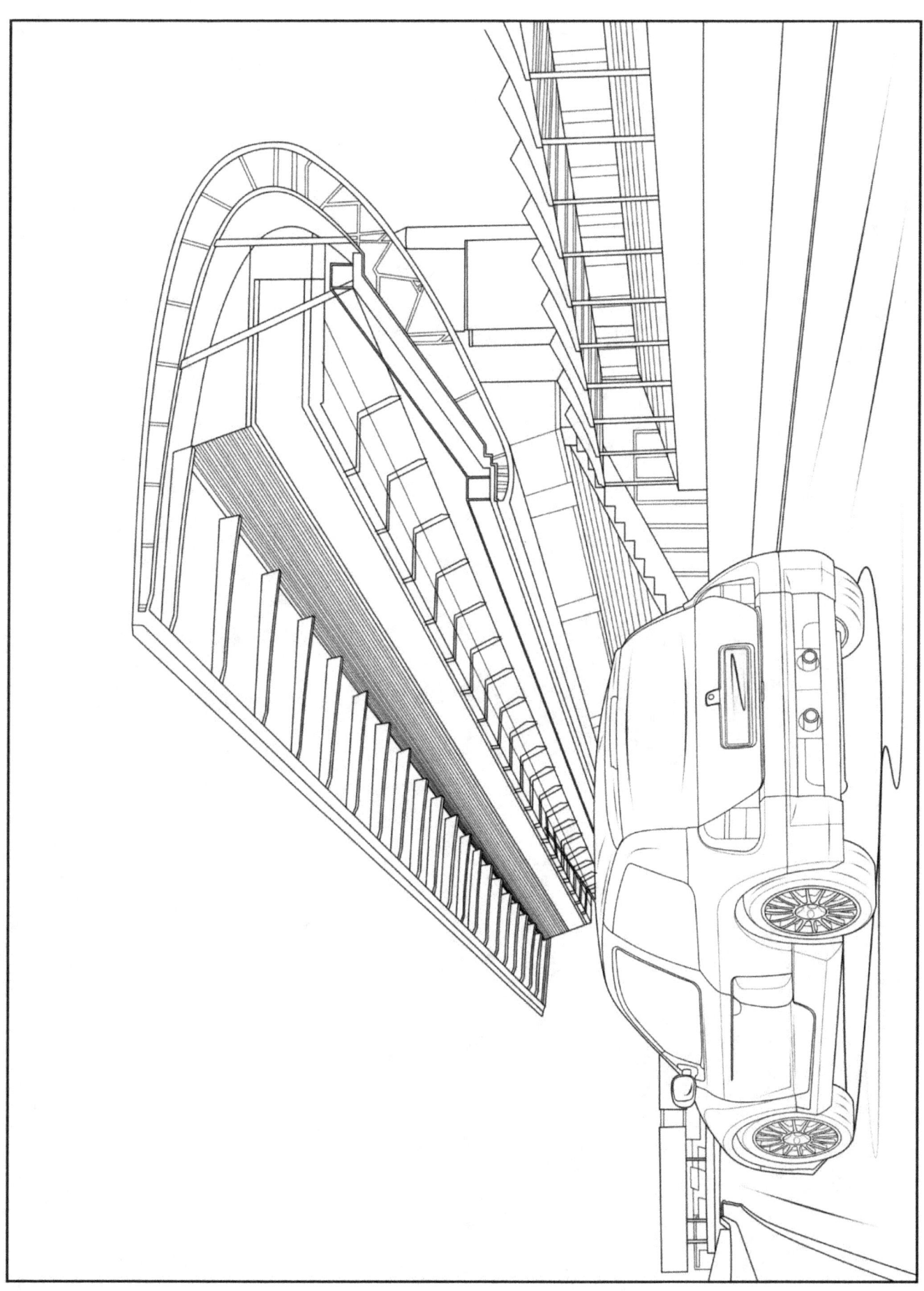

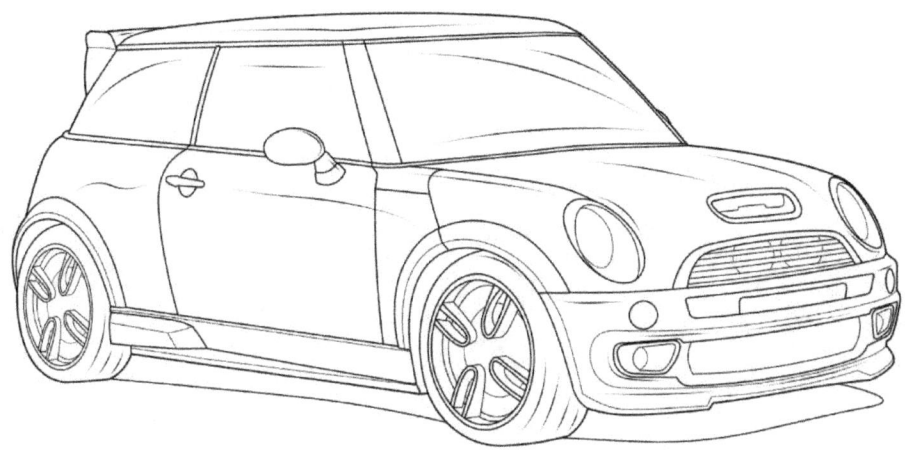

MINI JCW GP (2006)

The MINI Hardtop or 'MINI Hatch' as it's known in Europe was first launched in late 2000. It is owned by BMW Group who retained the MINI brand from their acquisition of The Rover Group from British Aerospace in 1994. A clever move, as the original MINI was an instant hit since it was first launched in 1959 all the way through to the end of its production in October 2000. The original MINI remains a popular British icon to this day.

In its early years the MINI Hardtop was available as a MINI One, MINI One D (diesel), MINI Cooper, MINI Cooper S and as a MINI JCW (John Cooper Works) model. It wasn't until the first generation was coming to the end of its life cycle that the MINI GP was introduced. The MINI GP is a track focused limited-edition model (limited to 2,000 units worldwide). It runs the same supercharged engine as the standard JCW model, but it featured many weight reducing measures such as the removal of the rear seats (substituted by an additional support brace in their place) and rear wash-wipe system. Under the hood (bonnet) it had a less restrictive intercooler, a re-worked engine management system, improved fuel injectors and a freer flowing exhaust system. For the exterior, the MINI GP was only available in 'Thunder' Grey metallic paint and it had a huge rear wing to help with air flow and down force.

There was a second version of the MINI GP released in 2012 and there is now a third incarnation of this cult car which has over 300 bhp! Still, the MINI GP1 remains as one of the best handling MINIs to this day and will remain as a highly desirable car due to the original limited production run.

Engine Size:	1,598 cc / 97.5 cu in
Power:	215 bhp
0-60:	5.9 seconds
Max Speed:	149 mph
Weight:	1,090 kg / 2,403 lbs

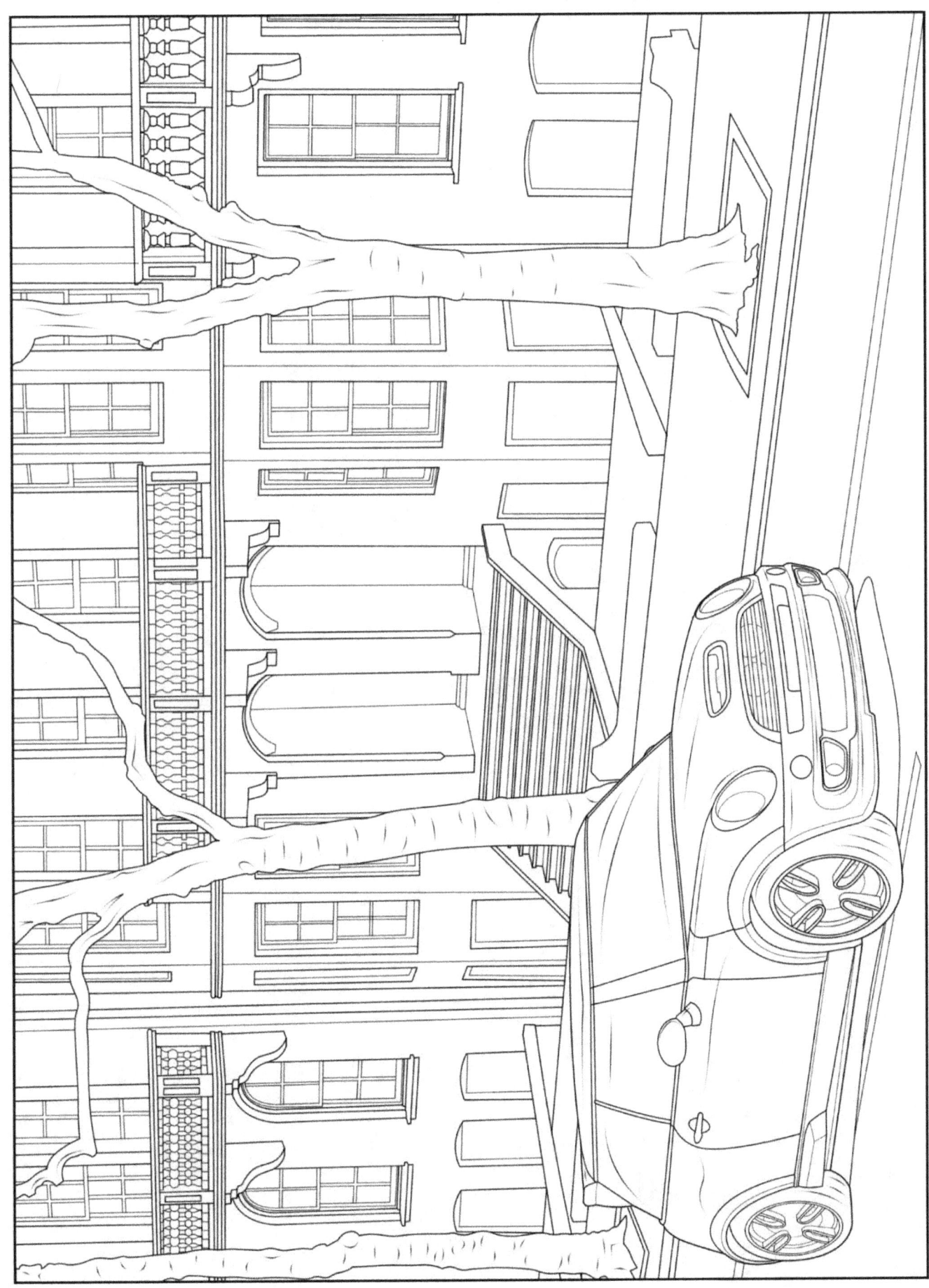

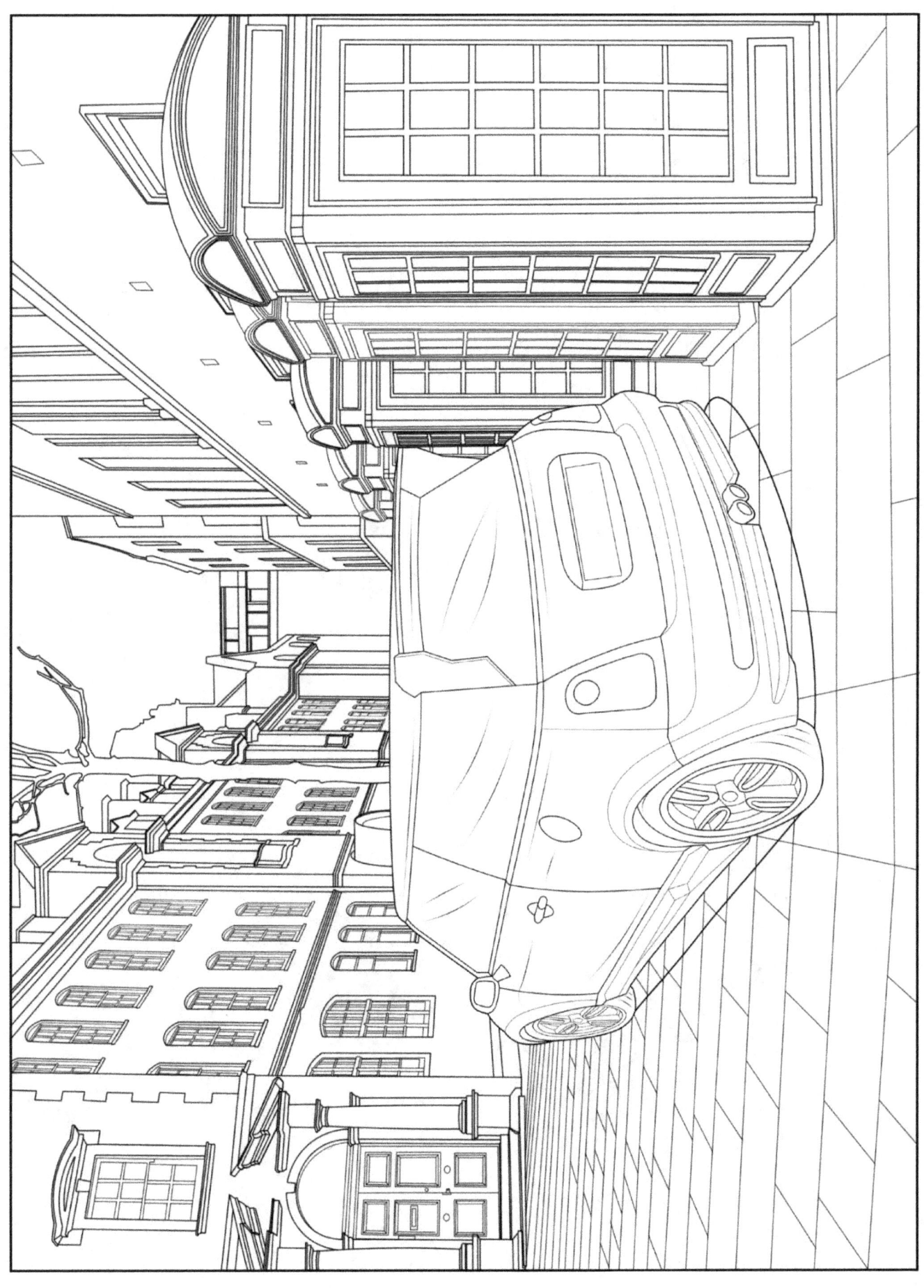

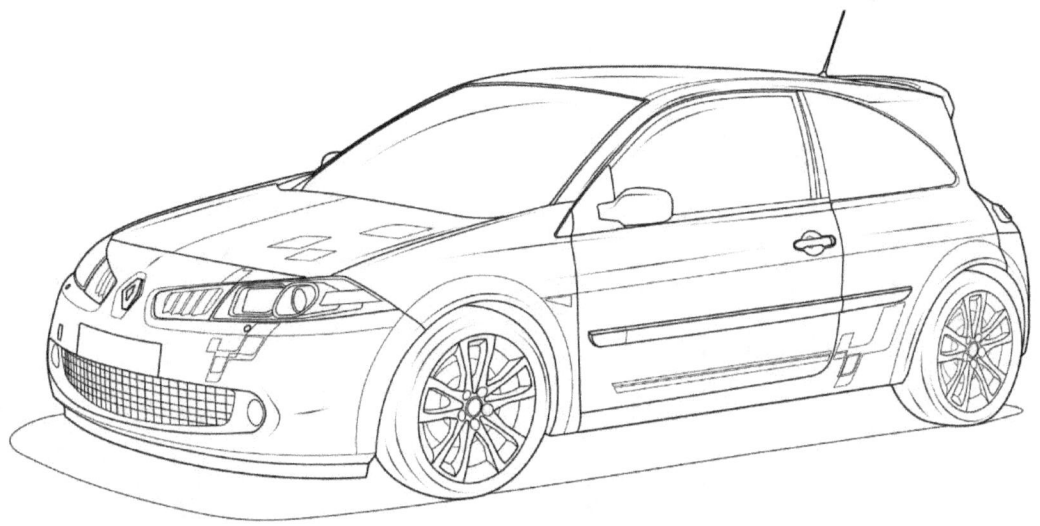

Renault Sport Mégane R26.R (2009)

The R26.R ('R' standing for 'Radical') was a totally stripped-down version of the already pretty light (and incredibly fast) R26 model.

The R26.R engineers were told that they weren't allowed to squeeze any more power from the engine. The only way to increase performance would be to 'add' lightness. They achieved this by removing the rear seats, passenger airbag (incl. curtain airbags), climate control, rear wash wipe, heated rear window, front fog lamps, headlamp washers, radio and most of the sound deadening. The hood (bonnet) was replaced with one made from carbon fiber and it received polycarbonate fenders (wings) side windows and tailgate. Upgraded springs, brake discs, and alloy wheels and Toyo tyres completed the handling upgrades. All these weight reducing measures made the R26.R a huge 123 kg lighter than the standard R26 model.

At launch the R26.R set a record for a front wheel drive car of 8 minutes 17.54 seconds around the Nordschleife section of the Nürburgring beating the previous record set by an Opel Astra GTC OPC (known as a Vauxhall Astra VXR in the UK or as a Holden VXR in Australia) by more than 19 seconds.

Like many of the cars featured in this book, production was limited. The R26.R was limited to 450 units worldwide which means that the Renault Sport Mégane R26.R will remain not only as one of the most track-focused hot hatches ever, but a hugely desirable collector's piece for years to come.

Engine Size:	1,998 cc / 121.9 cu in
Power:	230 bhp
0-60:	5.9 seconds
Max Speed:	143 mph
Weight:	1,232 kg / 2,716 lb

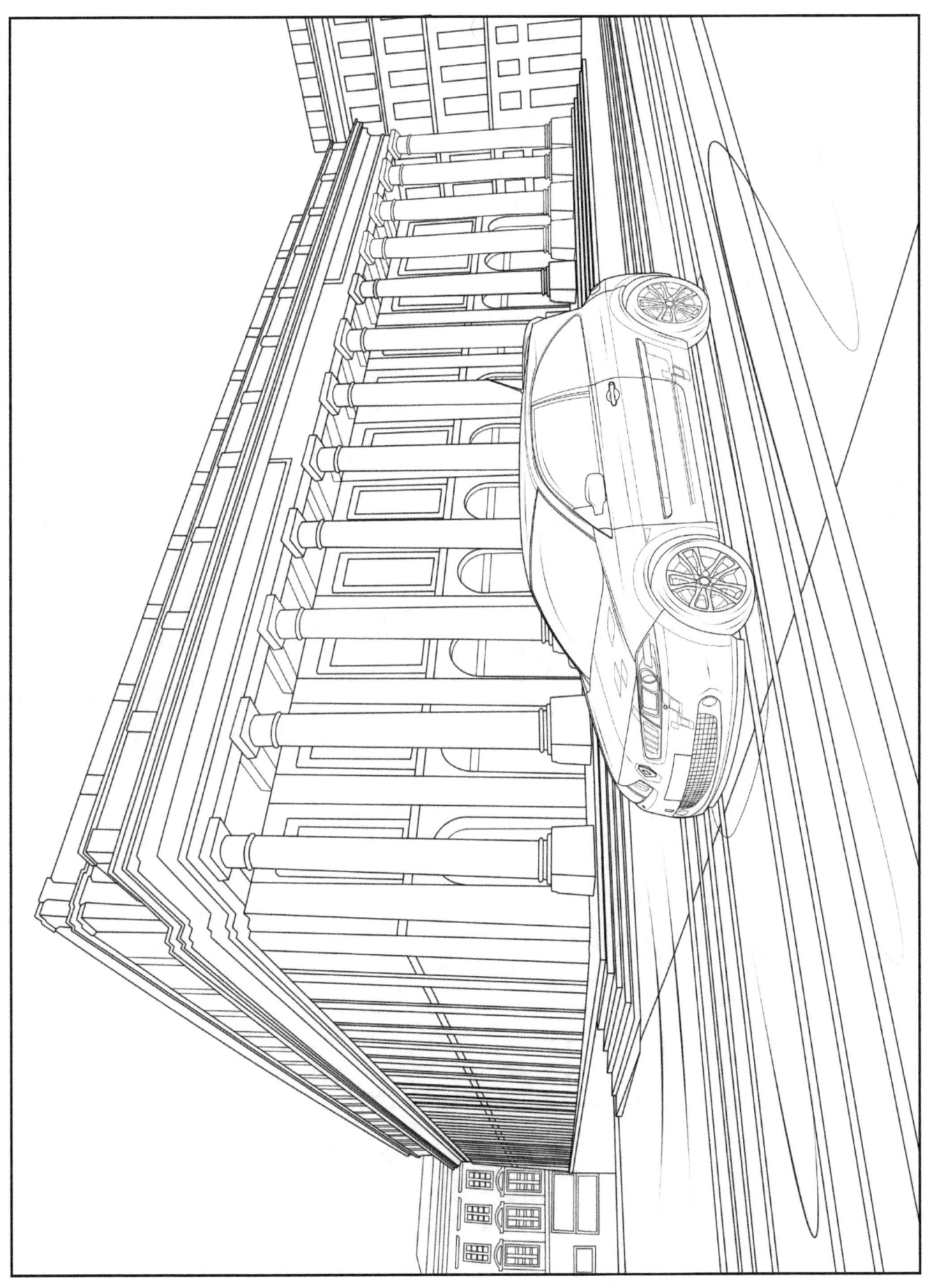

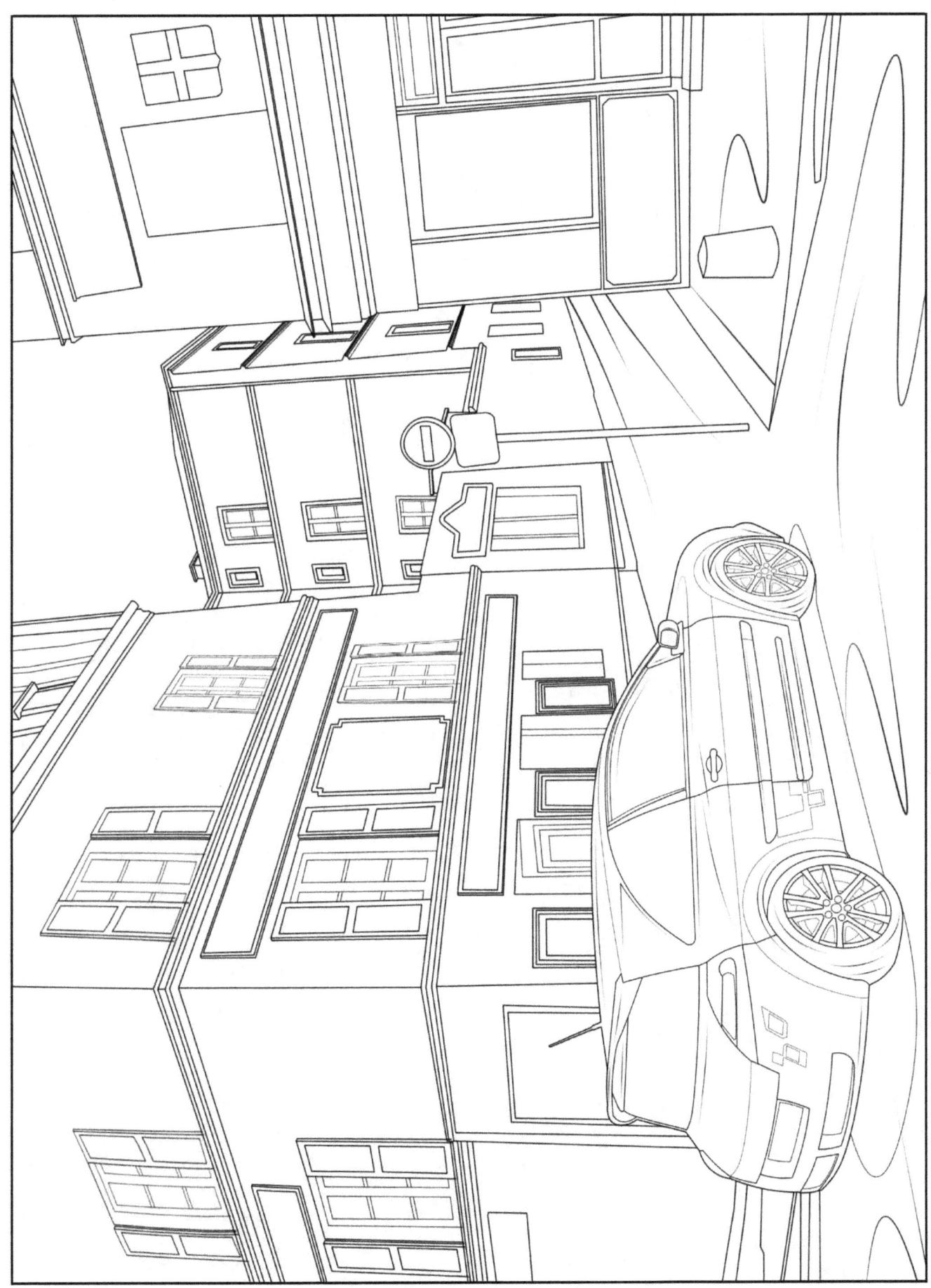

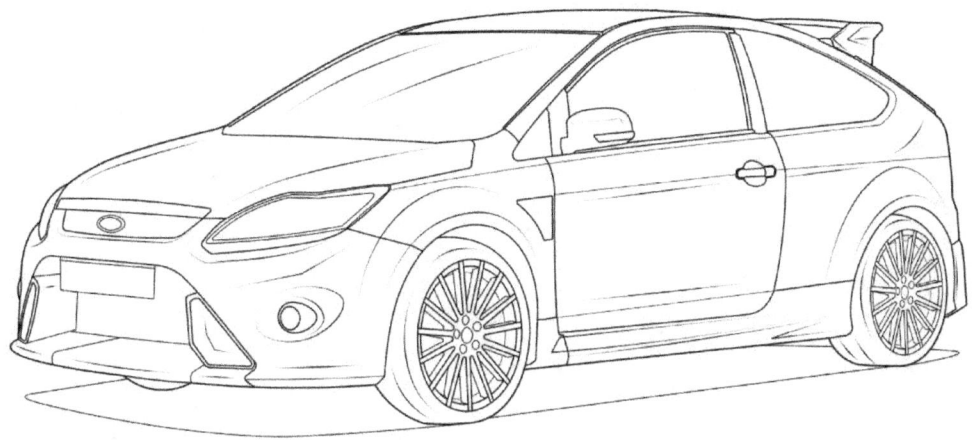

Ford Focus RS500 (2010)

The Ford Focus was the successor to the ever-popular Ford Escort which was a small family car produced by Ford Europe from 1968 to 2004.

The first Focus RS model ('RS' standing for 'Rallye Sport') came along in 2002 and featured a powerful 2.0 litre Duratec engine, limited slip differential, upgraded brakes, and significantly more aggressive body styling. It was only available as a front wheel drive, much to the dismay of many Ford purists who wanted a four-wheel drive set up like its predecessor – the Escort RS Cosworth. It, however, became an instant classic and has remained a hot hatch icon with serious rally pedigree ever since.

The second generation of Focus RS came along in 2009 and, like its forebearer, featured a conventional front-wheel drive layout, but power came from a Volvo sourced 2.5 litre Duratec engine that also powered the lesser Focus ST. Engine upgrades though came in their droves, and the final power output of the RS model was 301 hp which afforded the Focus RS a 0-60 time of 5.9 seconds and a top speed of 163 mph.

The RS500 was a limited production run (only 500 units were produced) and it only came in matte black (it was a matte black wrap over black paint). Power was, yet again, increased thanks to tuning from Mountune which upped the power to a very significant 345 bhp which added another 2 mph to the top speed and reduced the 0-60 dash by half a second. The Focus RS is a true rally car for the road and offers a truly rewarding driving experience if you are lucky enough to ever drive one.

Engine Size:	2,521 cc / 153.9 cu in
Power:	345 bhp
0-60:	5.4 seconds
Max Speed:	165 mph
Weight:	1,450 kg / 3,197 lbs

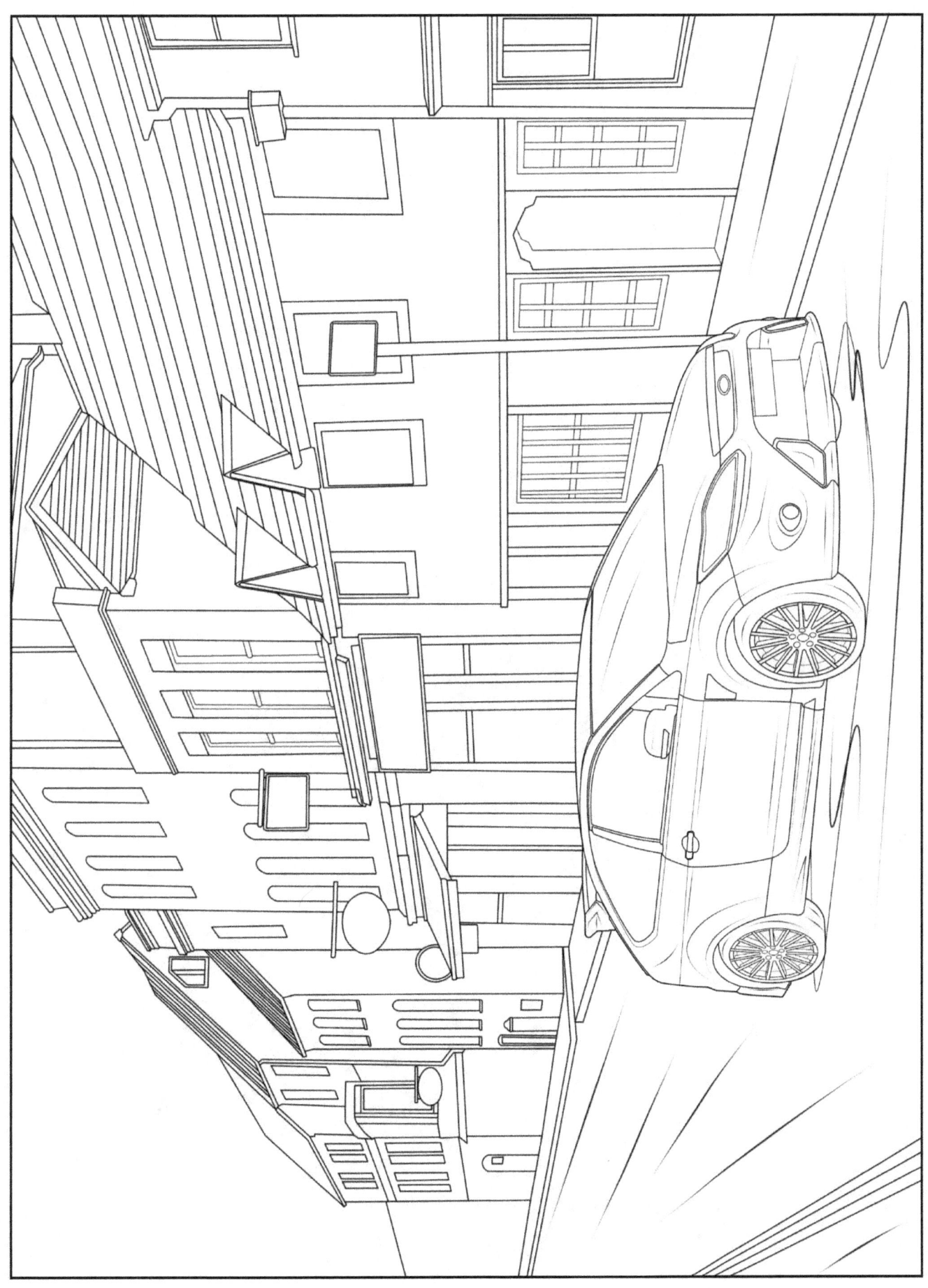

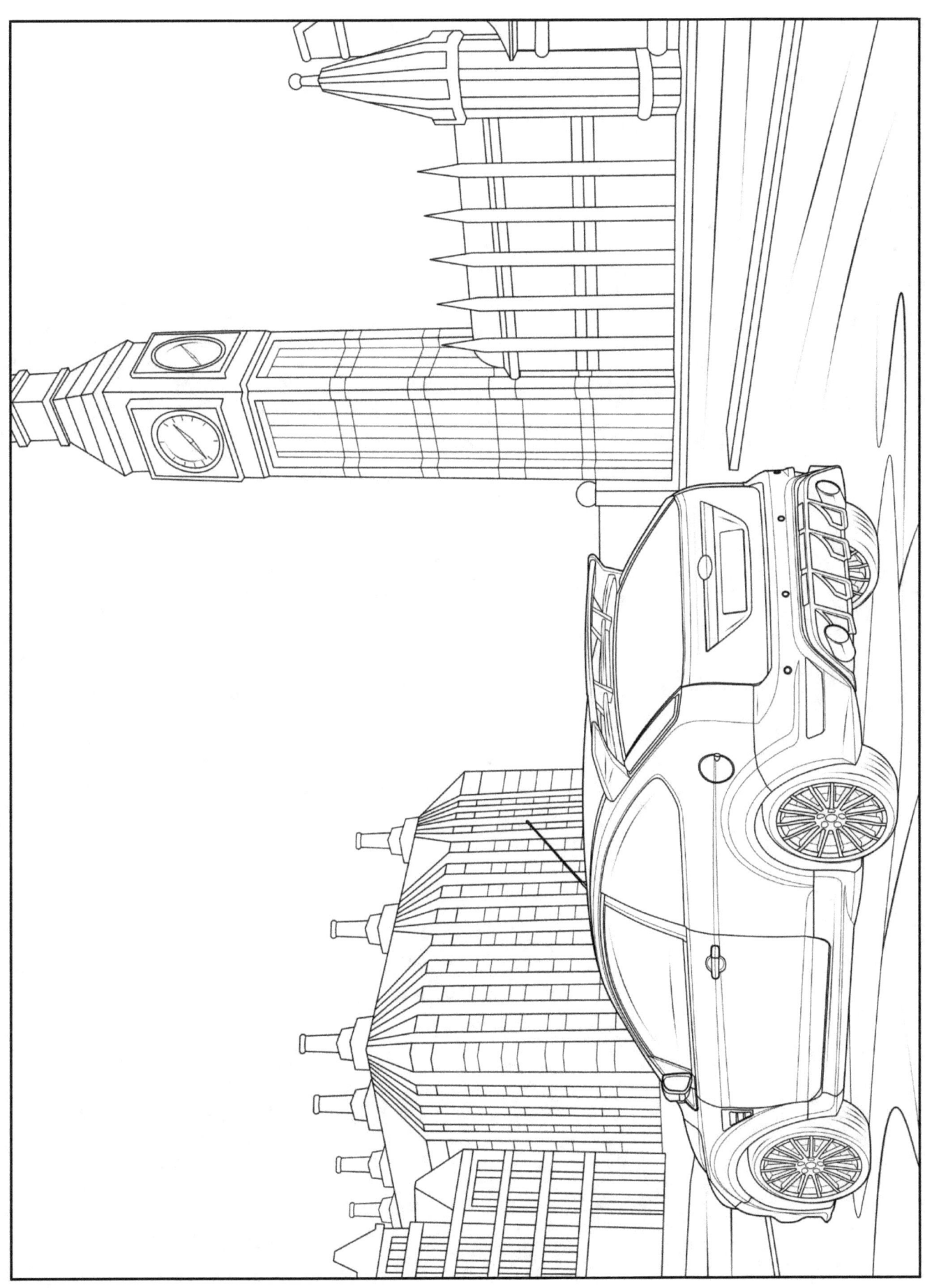

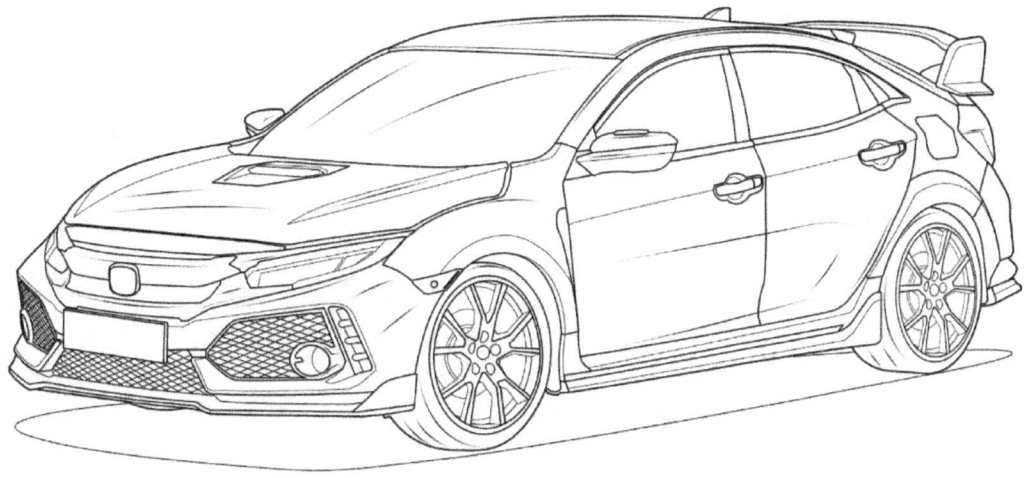

Honda Civic Type-R FK8 (2017)

The Honda Civic, now in its tenth generation has been Honda's hot hatch offering since the sixth generation EK9 model from 1997 (this model was only available in Japan).

Like many other hot hatches, the Type R is treated to stiffened suspension, a tuned engine, modified body styling, upgraded brakes and chassis, and a red Honda badge! The EK9 Type R also shared many of its components with the Honda Integra Type R of the same era. Along with the usual weight saving measures, one of the most notable characteristics of the original Type R models was the hand ported 'B16B' engine which boasted one of the highest power outputs per litre for a naturally aspirated car. This engine was an absolute screamer and really rewarded the driver when pushed to its 8,400-rpm red line.

The FK8 Type R continues the trend of using a high revving engine, however, it now benefits from addition turbo charged power and 316 bhp. This well-rehearsed recipe, along with the chassis and body styling afforded the FK8 Type R to achieve a Nordschleife Nürburgring time of 7 minutes 43.8 seconds which was a record when the car was first released. This time has since been surpassed by the Renault Mégane RS Trophy-R from 2019.

Engine Size:	1,996 cc / 121.8 cu in
Power:	316 bhp
0-60:	5.5 seconds
Max Speed:	169 mph
Weight:	1,380 kg / 3,042 lbs

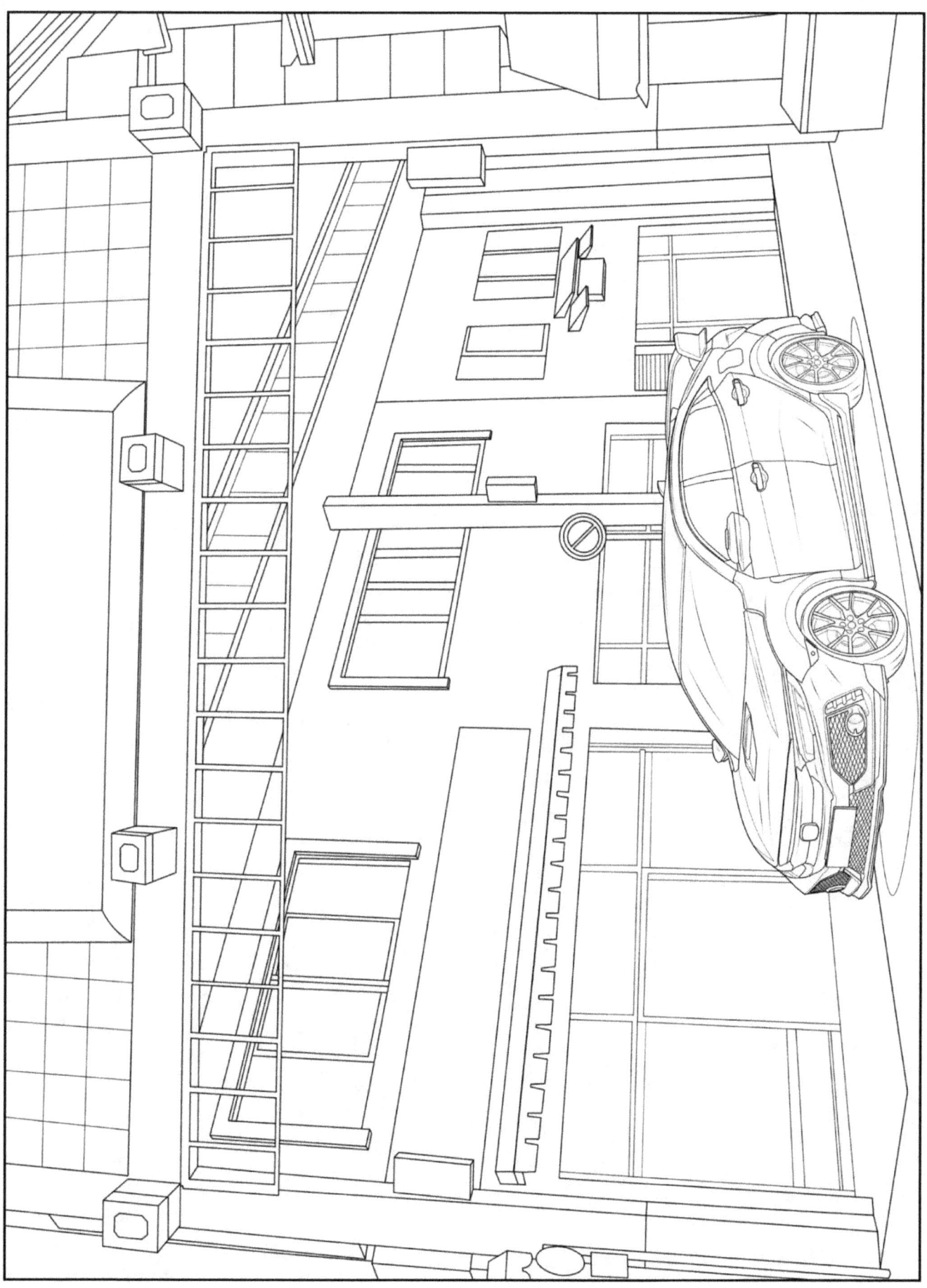

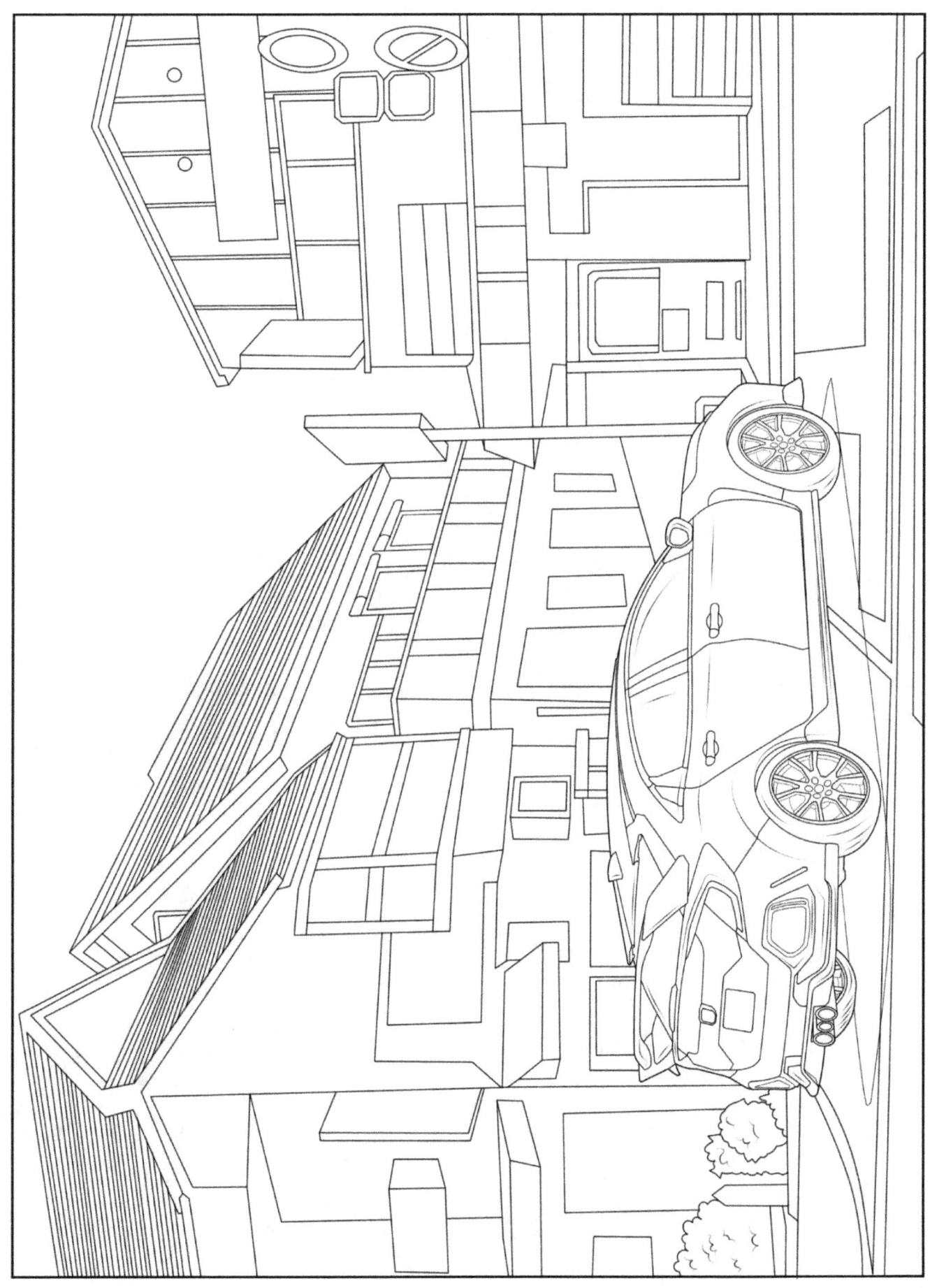

PLEASE SEE MY OTHER GREAT TITLES IN THIS SERIES!

Greatest American Muscle Cars Coloring Book – Modern Edition.
Includes the following:

- Dodge Challenger SRT Hellcat
- Chevrolet Camaro ZL1
- Ford Mustang Shelby GT 500
- Cadillac CTS-V
- Equus Bass 770
- Ford GT
- Dodge RAM SRT-10
- Jeep Grand Cherokee SRT Trackhawk
- Ford F-150 Raptor
- Dodge Charger SRT Hellcat 'Widebody'
- Chevrolet Corvette Z06
- Dodge Viper

Greatest American Muscle Cars Coloring Book – Classic Edition.
Includes the following:

- Shelby Mustang GT 500 KR
- Pontiac Tempest Le Mans GTO
- Buick GSX Stage 1
- Ford Mustang Boss 302
- Chevrolet Malibu SS Chevelle
- Dodge Charger R/T SE
- Oldsmobile 4-4-2
- Plymouth Road Runner
- Pontiac Firebird Trans Am
- Shelby Cobra 427
- Chevrolet Camaro IROC-Z
- Chevrolet Corvette 'Stingray'

The World's Most Iconic Cars Coloring Book.
Includes the following:

- Ford Model T
- MINI
- Citroen DS
- Jaguar E-Type
- Volkswagen Beetle
- Mercedes-Benz 300 SL
- Chevrolet Bel-Air
- Toyota 2000 GT
- Porsche 911 Carrera 2.7 RS
- Ferrari LaFerrari
- Lamborghini Miura P400
- Duesenberg Model J
- Aston Martin DB5
- Lamborghini Countach
- Ferrari 250 GTO

A small favor

Hello again, and thanks for purchasing The World's Best Hot Hatches Coloring Book! I really hope you had a great time relaxing and appreciating the awesome cars that I have carefully selected for inclusion in this book.

Whilst you're here I want to take this opportunity to tell you a little bit about myself. I worked in the motor industry for over 20 years (in car sales) as I truly have a deep and in-built passion for everything that involves cars. Most of my waking hours are spent thinking about cars. Hell, I even dream about them sometimes too! I did, however, decide to call it a day on my selling career in 2019 to focus my efforts on my coloring books. This is book number 4 in this series and there are more to come! Please feel free to check them out too.

If you enjoyed this book, please do take the time to give an honest Amazon review and share your experience with your friends and families. I read all the reviews and each review inspires me to keep producing great books for your coloring pleasure!

Thanks again for your purchase.

www.ingramcontent.com/pod-product-compliance
Lightning Source LLC
Chambersburg PA
CBHW080517220526
45465CB00006B/2515